Preface

---"25% of this book is not worth reading. I just don't know which 25%."—Jed Anderson

It's probably a different 25% for everyone. Please jump around this book if a particular thought is not resonating with you. That is how it was written. And that is how it is intended to be read.

I often don't feel as positive and motivated as the words in this book might sometimes sound. I often write because I need to read it myself. I hope these words might however give you courage and hope in your own storms—whatever they be—and a sense of a greater love that seems to be at work on this big ball down here.

The following is a collection of thoughts and writings over the last 10 years on a journey to reform the Clean Air Act. My experience with the Clean Air Act began in 1998 as a new attorney at a large law firm in Texas. After a few years helping clients navigate the Clean Air Act, I began to question its efficiency and effectiveness. It seemed too complicated. It seemed too redundant. It seemed too disjointed. I was making money—but I questioned the way in which I was making it. Why should my clients and the environment be subjected to so much unnecessary complexity which in the end seemed to be benefiting me more than anyone?

Four general themes are at work in this book. One is our innate abilities to overcome the false barriers of the world—including problems with the Clean Air Act. The second is the over-complexity of the air quality management system and the power of simplification. The third is the idea of pursuing a more holistic approach to air quality and climate change concerns rather than the current overlapping, single-pollutant, fragmented approach. The final theme is that air pollution is no longer primarily a local problem as it largely was 40 years ago when the Clean Air Act was originally written. The world has grown up around us. Our understanding of the global and interactive nature of pollutants has also matured. Responsibility for a

particular facet of a problem must be aligned with the authority to solve that part of the problem in order for a system to properly work.

It's become a "small multi-pollutant world after all." It's time to simplify and transform the Clean Air Act to better prepare ourselves for the problems and opportunities of a 21st century world. We can make this happen.

It has been a joy to be on this journey to transform the Clean Air Act. It truly has been a "victorious defeat."

Light and the Clean Air Act

Some people don't want to draw attention to themselves because they don't want others thinking, "Boy, that person sure thinks they are wonderful."

What's wrong with looking like you are wonderful? You are wonderful.

How is the world improved by not letting your light shine?

The goal is not to be better than others. Or to be better than one's self. But to be better than self. Putting a bushel on the light isn't modesty—it's selfishness. It's in truth an unwillingness to abandon self and become translucent to the light.

Time to let your light shine.

> -----"We must let our light shine, make our faith, our hope, our love manifest—that men may praise, not us for shining, but the Father for creating the light."—George MacDonald

Consensus

How do we get consensus on how to update the Clean Air Act? Quite easy. Just a matter of personally searching for the truth as best we can see it. I will explain.

Our objective on every issue should be to search beyond ourselves for the truth in a particular issue as best we can see it. The harder we seek this truth for ourselves in everything, the closer we will eventually get to the same or similar solution since we are all seeking the same thing—the truth. Anyone remember "Where's Waldo"? The reason we found him is we were all looking for the same thing. Eventually there was consensus on where Waldo was. What if the game though was called "Where's Consensus"? I think we would still be looking for Consensus.

Each of us is designed to find Waldo. The more we search for the truth in any particular issue the more we realize we are looking for the same thing

and the closer we get to finding the same thing. And that same thing we will one day find will just be wonderful. . . . It's the truth.

Perspective

Sometimes we think of the Clean Air Act as this venerable, imposing, indomitable force. Just some perspective I wanted to share. Each one of you is far more powerful and important than the Clean Air Act. I think we tend to believe the opposite. That is not the case and I will prove it. Eternity is not promised to statutes and institutions. Eternity is promised to you. The Clean Air Act will eventually die. You won't. You are therefore far more powerful and important than the Clean Air Act will ever be.

Improving the Clean Air Act doesn't seem as imposing anymore does it? . . . especially for a creature who will one day remember the Clean Air Act and the galaxies as an old tale.

Best way to Protect Nature

The best way to protect nature is to emulate nature.

-----"Nature operates in the shortest way possible." — Aristotle

-----"Nature is pleased with simplicity. And nature is no dummy." — Isaac Newton

-----"Nature does not multiply things unnecessarily . . . and does nothing in vain". — Galileo

Sacred vs. Secular

People tell me I keep jumbling up religion and science and philosophy and public policy and theology.

All seem related. All seem to draw from and point to the same source. I'm a strong advocate of the separation of Church and State, but to separate the sacred from the secular would seem to be an exercise in ecumenical futility. All seems sacred. Praying . . . engineering . . . all sacred.

I've never heard secular music. I've heard music with sins in it, but I've never heard secular music. Seems like a cosmic impossibility.

> -----"Life and religion are one, or neither is anything."–George MacDonald

Liberals, Conservatives, and the Clean Air Act

Liberals are not thinking liberal enough on this issue yet. And the conservatives are not thinking conservative enough.

Let's end both pollution and environmental laws.

It's not idealism. Just pragmatism with an extended timeline.

It's Better to Fail

I failed again at requesting that the State of Texas recognize foreign pollution impacts to our health, economy, and ability to achieve air quality standards.

I don't want the truth to fail, whatever that is, but it's better for us personally to fail. How can I say this? Well, I think a'Kempis was on to something:

> -----"Sorrow always accompanies the world's glory. [. . .] Those who seek temporal glory or do not despise it with their hearts, show that they have little love for the glory of heaven. The person who cares nothing about the approval or disapproval of people enjoys great peace of mind. If your conscience is pure you will easily be satisfied and restored to peace. You are not more holy when you are praised, or more worthless when you are disparaged. You are what you are, and you cannot be said to be greater than what you are in the sight of God. If you consider what you are within you, then you will not be concerned about what people say about you. "People look at the outward appearance, but the Lord looks at the heart." They consider the deeds a person does, but God considers the motives." To be always doing well and have little regard for yourself is the sign of a humble soul. It is a sign of great purity and inward confidence

not to look for comfort from any person. Those who seek not witness outside themselves, show that they have fully committed themselves to God. "For it is not those who commend themselves that are approved," says Paul, "but those whom the Lord commends". Spiritual people walk inward with God and are not sustained by any outward feelings."–Thomas a' Kempis

Failure seems to be one of the only cures for the pride and selfishness that many of us struggle with—and the cattle prod to seeking the more likely source of the peace we so desperately desire. And so, though we might say this in a half-wincing, half-cowering voice . . . "bring it on".

—- "The phoenix must burn to emerge." – Janet Fitch

New Year's Resolutions

Many people say, "Why make resolutions I'm likely to fail at anyway?"

Not the point. God works from intent—not probability of success.

Problem isn't that we make resolutions that are impossible, but that they are not impossible enough.

The Call for Clean Air Act Transformation

Some may think of the Clean Air Act transformation effort as rebellious. Nothing could be further from the truth. Is the alcoholic rebellious for deciding to do something other than drink?

What is truly rebellious is to know that something is no longer good for you . . . and to keep doing it. That is truly rebellious.

If we engage in the Clean Air Act transformation effort out of love for our nation and a belief that we can do better, then we are calling on the same human nature that led to the creation of this great nation. It is this nature that calls us forward to improvement. It is this nature we cannot ignore.

Belief and the Clean Air Act

"I believe I can change the Clean Air Act." When I tell people this they look at me like I just told them I believed I could fly to Neptune.

Some people mistakenly think that belief is a feeling. That one must feel like they believe in order to believe. Belief is not a feeling. Belief is a choice. Feelings come and go. Feelings are fickle. Nothing can be built on a feeling of belief. Mountains can be built on a choice of belief.

The Weak or the Strong?

Do you think it will take a strong powerful organization to reform the Clean Air Act? Do you think a small person such as yourself has no chance? You are absolutely wrong. It is the exact opposite. What do you think would have happened if the Israelites sent out their strongest man to meet Goliath? Just picture a strong man being sent out from the Israelite's skirmishing lines—walking with heavy armor and sword slowly toward Goliath. Goliath would have undoubtedly perceived this man a threat. Goliath would have had all kinds of time to prepare. Instead Goliath sees a small boy. And the only thing this boy's got is a sling-shot. And this kids running at him!! What the heck is this kid doing Goliath must have thought?! What a joke! I imagine by the time Goliath put two-and-two together the stone was about three feet from his forehead.

You and I have a much greater chance of reforming the Clean Air Act than the strong and powerful of this world. I hope if anything I can convince you of this. It's the Davids that are not anticipated. It's the small starfighter flying at the Death Star that no one expects. Strength is manifest in weakness. And when a problem is insurmountable the only way to attack it really is through weakness. You might not feel strong enough for this challenge, I certainly don't, but the good thing is we don't need to. Just switch off the targeting computer. Fly by faith. If it's the right thing to do then just do it and trust that all will be well— because it will be. It's the one unfailing principle.

-------"Never doubt that a small, group of thoughtful, committed citizens can change the world. Indeed, it is the only thing that ever has." - Margaret Mead

Trying

Not as important that we succeed. Only that we try. The goal as far as I can see it isn't to leave this earth with a list of accomplishments and a medal around our neck. The goal is to leave with as many scars as possible and a smile on our face.

The Lorax and the Clean Air Act

"But now," says the Once-ler,
"Now that you're here,
The word of the Lorax seems perfectly clear.
UNLESS someone like you cares a whole awful lot,
Nothing is going to get better.
It's not."

"SO . . .
Reform the Clean Air Act!" calls the Once-ler.
"We can't do things the same.
The world is changing, we need a new game.
Pollution is coming from foreign sources
States need new recourses for these sources of courses."

"Our future is looking just as bright as can be
Let's create some new soil for this Truffula Tree
To grow, and to green—Clean Air Act reform will soon provide
More clean air, more thneeds—for everyone world-wide."

"So let's jump in there and try this reform will we succeed?
98 and ¾ percent guaranteed!"

Idealism

"I admire your idealism . . ."

An audience member during the last Clean Air Act reform presentation I made prefaced a comment in this way.

Idealistic? Clean air Act reform? As strange as this might initially sound, the most pragmatic thing I've been involved with is Clean Air Act reform. The most idealistic endeavor has been engaging in the Clean Air Act with the hope that air quality will be timely and cost-effectively improved.

I think we sometimes confuse pragmatism with idealism when pragmatism requires more than a couple day's effort.

Time to transform the Clean Air Act. Time to venture forth. We have not been designed for the harbor. We have been designed for the sea. All will be well.

Attribution

99% of my best work is plagiarism.

Power and Influence

We don't need more power and influence to improve the Clean Air Act—just more love. This is not mushy sentiment. It's practical business-like advice. I will explain.

> -----"Love feels no burden, thinks nothing of trouble, attempts what is above its strength, does not complain about impossibility, for it thinks all things lawful for itself, and all things possible. It is therefore able to undertake all things and complete many of them and cause them to take effect— where the person who does not love would faint and give up." –Thomas a'Kempis

Many people have fainted and given up—or not started. Many others like myself have faltered. What's needed to overcome this is not more power and influence, but as explained above, more love. And this is quite easy to get. I've read the only thing we need to do is ask.

What's in this Reform Effort for us Personally?

This might seem strange, but I think we are already receiving our reward. When the Clean Air Act is updated and simplified I think it will be a great day for the environment, industry, and our nation—but it will be a sad day for those working to help make it happen. Satisfaction and growth lies in effort. And failure seems to be a much fairer friend than success. Our aspiration, whether we are cognizant of it or not, seems to me to be made greater than ourselves—to which effort and failure appear to be the better teachers.

> —"To be made greater than one's fellows is the offered reward of hell, and involves no greatness; to be made greater than one's self, is the divine reward, and involves a real greatness."—George MacDonald

We've got a long way to go, but what a beautiful gift we are being given.

Clean Air Act Reform is Easy

People wonder why I think Clean Air Act reform is relatively so easy. It's because I've tried Jed reform.

The World's Judgment and the Clean Air Act

The world is saying that the Clean Air Act can't be fixed—and even if it could be fixed—you are too small, weak, old, young, broken, ill-positioned, or insignificant to do anything about it.

Who's voice are you going to listen to? The world's?

> -----"The world is not so excellent that its judgment of greatness unequivocally has great significance – except as unconscious sarcasm."—Soren Kierkegaard

Simplifying the Air Quality Management System

We must simplify the air quality management system in the United States. With simplicity comes transparency. With transparency comes accountability. The more simple things are, the more everyone understands them. The more everyone understands them, the more they comply with them. It's that simple.

Apologetics on Clean Air Act Reform

I hope everyone has figured out that about 75% of what I say is hooey and about 25% is good stuff. Unfortunately I can't differentiate the two. I therefore leave it to you to figure out which is which. What matters is that truth is advanced—whatever that is. I for whatever reason feel compelled to share the truth on this as best as I see it. If I'm proven wrong that will be fine. I will be dust. Just a fact. Truth will endure. I will be gone. What matters is therefore truth. And frankly the last thing I need is to be right about anything since I'm in such a constant battle with pride and self. My biggest impediment to what I'm looking for is clearly not Congress, but Jed. If any of you think that Clean Air Act reform is hard, try Jed reform!

All will be well. Thank you all for your tolerance, patience, and for helping to seek and advance the truth on all this. What a fun journey it is.

The Goal

No more pollution. No more environmental laws. And for companies to make billions of dollars making wonderful products for us to use and enjoy.

It won't be tomorrow. But it will be some tomorrow.

Music and the Clean Air Act

Think the foundations of the Clean Air Act need to remain long and complicated to handle the complex, nuanced, and multifarious world we now live in?

Most music as we know it only uses 12 notes. From Rachmaninoff to Bob Marley, from Muddy Waters to Eminem—only 12 notes.

Despite the almost astronomical complexity, creativity, memories, feelings, thoughts, and ideas for which music has been responsible for generating—only 12 notes have ever been used.

Imagine the music we could play with a simplified Clean Air Act. Let's make it happen.

Change

Many people don't want to change the Clean Air Act because they think that whatever we get from Congress will be worse than what we already have.

- Who has made a change for the worse in their life?
- Who has made a change for the better?
- Which is more often the result?

I think we will one day look back on our life and see that most of our mistakes were not commissions—but omissions. It will not be the bad things we did, but the good things we didn't. It will not be our changes, but our lack of changes that will trouble us most.

-----"Twenty years from now you will be more disappointed by the things that you didn't do than by the ones you did do. So throw off the bowlines. Sail away from the safe harbor. Catch the trade winds in your sails. Explore. Dream. Discover."—Mark Twain

Best Place for Tackling the Impossible

Go sit in the woods or your closet for an hour.

The world will tell you that you just wasted an hour.

Eternity and the results I think might eventually tell you otherwise.

Simplicity and the Clean Air Act

The reason things are still complicated is that we do not fully understand them. Once we fully understand them . . . they will become simple.

It fascinates me how Einstein and other brilliant minds throughout the centuries have been absolutely obsessed with simplicity. As Einstein said, "When the solution is simple, God is answering." Einstein's breakthrough in the theory of relativity came not from adding additional complexity to the mathematical equation, but from simplification. When other scientists were racking their brains trying to calculate aether using the Lorentz transformation, Einstein had the gall to ask "why calculate it?"—and dropped aether from the equation. The theory of special relativity was born. Shocking. Absolutely brilliant.

Einstein in fact was so obsessed with simplicity that he spent the last 30 years of his life in relative obscurity trying to simplify the rules that govern the universe into one unified theory. Einstein believed that "God does not play dice with the universe"—and that nothing happened by chance. Disappointment plagued Einstein throughout the latter years of his life, but he could not let go of his belief that there was one simple answer to everything. Even on his death bed he was scribbling mathematical calculations that would unite the theories of gravitation and electromagnetism.

Fascinating. Makes you wonder what treasures we might discover if we tried to simplify the Clean Air Act.

Accepting Things as They Are

It sometimes might seem easier to just accept problems with the Clean Air Act and the problems we face in life as they are. Some words of George McDonald I read this morning that I wanted to share:

> -----"Of all things let us avoid the false refuge of a weary collapse, a hopeless yielding to things as they are. It is the life in us that is discontented; we need more of what is discontented, not more of the cause of its discontent. Discontent, I repeat, is the life in us that has not enough of itself, is not enough to itself, so calls for more. He has the victory who, in the midst of pain and weakness, cries out, not for death, not for the repose of forgetfulness, but for strength to fight; for more power, more consciousness of being, more God in him; who, when sorest wounded, says with Sir Andrew Barton in the old ballad:— Fight on my men, says Sir Andrew Barton, I am hurt,

but I am not slain; I'll lay me down and bleed awhile, And then I'll rise and fight again; —and that with no silly notion of playing the hero—what have creatures like us to do with heroism who are not yet barely honest!—but because so to fight is the truth, and the only way."

Let's lay down and bleed for a while if we need to. Then rise and fight again.

You or Congress

I believe many of you stand a greater chance of transforming the Clean Air Act than most Senators or Representatives. Does this sound crazy? Absolutely not. I will prove it. Here is an extreme example that proves my point. Who is more likely to hit a baseball in the following circumstance— an Albert Pujols who believes he can't hit the baseball and doesn't try . . . or a 6 year-old little leaguer who believes he can hit it? I'll take the 6 year-old every time—even if the situation looks impossible. It's not because the 6 year-old is more powerful than Albert Pujols. It's because the 6 year-old believes they can hit it and they are not afraid to swing at the ball—even if it's outside their strike-zone.

It's not that I believe you are more powerful than a Senator. The reason why I believe that many of you stand a greater chance of transforming the Clean Air Act than most Senators and Representatives is because you believe that the Clean Air Act can be transformed and you have the courage to act on this belief. I'll take the Davids of the world every time. You have much more potential than you likely realize.

> ----- "Thousands of geniuses live and die undiscovered -- either by themselves or by others." ---Mark Twain

Simplicity

I wonder what would happen if we applied Occam's Razor to Clean Air Act?

- "The Clean Air Act is a model of redundancy. Virtually every type of pollutant is regulated by not one but several overlapping provisions." - Ben Lieberman

- "I hate that each sector has 17 to 20 rules that govern each piece of equipment and you've got to be a neuroscientist to figure it out". --Gina McCarthy, U.S. EPA Administrator

Occam's Razor is that "entities are not to be multiplied beyond necessity." Occam—borrowing largely from Aristotle—posited the following:

(A) It is futile to do with more what can be done with fewer. [Frustra fit per plura quod potest fieri per pauciora.]
(B) When a proposition comes out true for things, if two things suffice for its truth, it is superfluous to assume a third. [Quando propositio verificatur pro rebus, si duae res sufficiunt ad eius veritatem, superfluum est ponere tertiam.]
(C) Plurality should not be assumed without necessity. [Pluralitas non est ponenda sine necessitate.]
(D) No plurality should be assumed unless it can be proved (a) by reason, or (b) by experience, or (c) by some infallible authority. [Nulla pluralitas est ponenda nisi per rationem vel experientiam vel auctoritatem illius, qui non potest falli nec errare, potest convinci.]

In physics, Occam's Razor (or parsimony) was used to formulate the theory of special relativity by Einstein, the principle of least action by Mauepertuis and Euler, and quantum mechanics by Planck, Heisenberg, and Broglie. In chemistry, Occam's razor was used to develop the theories of thermodynamics and the reaction mechanism. In statistics and probability theory: Occam's razor is part and parcel of the idea that if an assumption does not improve the accuracy of a theory, its only effect is to increase the probability that the overall theory is wrong. Several theories and explanations in this field have derived or expanded on Occam's razor including; Kolmogorov complexity, Bayesian model comparison, Akaike Information Criterion, Laplace approximation, and the Kolmogorov-Chaitin Minimum description length approach. In biology, Occam's razor was used in the development of evolutionary biology and systematics. In religion, Occam's Razor was used by Thomas Aquinas to help explain the existence of God. Aquinas was noted for saying, "If a thing can be done adequately by means of one, it is superfluous to do it by means of several; for we observe that nature does not employ two instruments [if] one suffices."

What would happen if we applied Occam's Razor to the Clean Air Act?

The world is changing. We must change with it. Time to transform the Clean Air Act. We can make it happen.

Two Duties

We are doctors. All of us are helping our patients with their air quality ailments—whether we represent industry, the environment, or government. This is a beautiful and critical service we provide. Our patients need our help with these day-to-day ailments—and it's great to get paid to help them. But we also have a another duty. That duty is to work toward the day that our patients will no longer need our help. When there is no more pollution. When there are no more environmental laws. When companies can make billions of dollars making all kinds of wonderful products for us to use and enjoy.

Let's keep reducing pollution and environmental laws until they are both gone.

------ "As soon as anyone starts telling you to be "realistic," cross that person off your invitation list." – John Eliot

Time to transform the Clean Air Act process. We can make it happen.

Clean Air Act Reform and the Little Engine that Could

We again appear to be at a crossroads with the Clean Air Act. We have a choice to make. The first is to ignore the issue and say "it's not my problem", "I've got more important things to do", or "I might get hurt". For those of you who've read the book "The Little Engine That Could", this is what the Shiny New Engine, the Big Strong Freight Engine, and the Tired Rusty Engine said. The second choice is to stand at the bottom of the mountain, a small and insignificant engine, knowing that you might get hurt, and start inching your way up that mountain.

I think we can. I think we can. I think we can. I think we can.

How can we Transform the Clean Air Act?

How can we transform the Clean Air Act? The key I think is not to focus on what Congress, EPA, or others should be doing. The most destructive

thinking is to sit there and say, "If Congress would only improve the Clean Air Act" or "if Administrator Jackson would only suggest to Congress that the Clean Air Act be improved". The only way we can transform the Clean Air Act I think is to focus on ourselves.

Anyone married? Anyone tried to change their spouse? Doesn't work does it? (If it does please call me and tell me what you did). I'm starting to learn that the best way to change my spouse is to change myself. Not only does this seem to work better, but it is much less frustrating and it gives me much more power and control over the situation. It also improves me—which is usually where the problem lies anyway. I think it works exactly the same when it comes to Congress. The best and easiest way to change them is to focus on ourselves and what we can do. This gives us power over the situation and the potential to succeed. Externalized problems never get solved. Internalized problems however at least have the potential of getting solved. That's why all problem solving I think must first start with a willingness to internalize the problem. And the great thing is that this internalization is far from being burdensome, but rather is quite freeing. Before our problems weighed us down because we could not solve them—they were outside ourselves. Now we potentially can solve them—they are within.

Time to internalize Clean Air Act problems and hold them up to the inner light. It is the only way to solve the problem. We can make it happen.

False Barriers

"I can't speak up about simplifying and improving the Clean Air Act . . . my job won't let me."

Fear can create all kinds of false barriers in our minds. 90% of fear lacks a basis . . . and 100% of fear lacks the truth.

> ------"Remembering that you are going to die is the best way I know to avoid the trap of thinking you have something to lose. You are already naked. There is no reason not to follow your heart." – Steve Jobs

How can I believe that you and I are capable of transforming the Clean Air Act?

Apparently some folks are asking this question and I thought I would answer it. How can I believe that you and I are capable of transforming the Clean Air Act? Am I crazy? Am I that arrogant? Am I that naïve? At least as far as I go I've got no power, authority, or position. I am a relative nobody—with considerable human shortfalls and frailties. All true. Yet I still believe that you and I can transform the Clean Air Act. How? Here is my rationale:

> 1. I am nothing.
> 2. In God all things are possible.
> 3. God works through you and I.

If I believed that you or I could transform the Clean Air Act based on a belief in myself I indeed would be crazy, arrogant, and naïve—but this is not the reason. The reason is that I believe that in God all things are possible and that God has no choice but to work through humanity. As Antonio Stradivari the famous violin maker once said, "God cannot make Stradivarius violins without Antonio Stradivari."

I've seen people with far less power and authority than you and I do much greater things in this world than transform the Clean Air Act. You and I are beautiful instruments—capable of anything I believe in the hands of the Virtuoso. You might be thinking that I think more highly of your capabilities than you do yourself, but I would hope you would at least consider the above rationale before you dismiss my belief in you as ill-fitted.

I hope this explains to you why I believe that you and I are capable of transforming the Clean Air Act. I'm not sure if or how we will be used, or whether we are being used in a given situation, but to believe that we can't be used because we are too small would be to place limits on God—which I can't do. There is too much evidence to the contrary.

Blame and the Clean Air Act

Who do I mostly blame for failing to update the Clean Air Act?

-----"If you could kick the person in the pants responsible for most of your trouble, you wouldn't sit for a month."–Theodore Roosevelt

The world is changing. We must change with it. Time to transform the Clean Air Act. We can make it happen.

The Pain and Difficulty of Transforming the Clean Air Act

The main reason why I think we don't want to get involved with updating the Clean Air Act is that it will be difficult and painful. We want happiness and peace—not pain and difficulty.

Fascinating thing though. Can't find happiness and peace by trying to avoid pain and difficulty. I've tried it. Doesn't work. Pain and difficulty are inevitable in this life. In fact, they seem to be the rule rather than the exception. Three options. One is to let the storms of life blow us where they will. Another is to try to avoid them—which we can't. The third is to say "so that's the way it's gonna be", put the bow into the waves, and start paddling.

Anyone see someone put their bow into a storm and eventually start smiling, laughing, and giving thanks for it? As much as you can find happiness and peace in this life—I think that person found it. And I bet they would tell you they would never have found this level of happiness and peace if it were not for the storm.

-----"I asked God for strength, that I might achieve, I was made weak, that I might learn humbly to obey. I asked God for health, that I might do greater things, I was given infirmity, that I might do better things. I asked for riches, that I might be happy, I was given poverty, that I might be wise. I asked for power, that I might have the praise of men, I was given weakness, that I might feel the need of God. I asked for all things, that I might enjoy life, I was given life, that I might enjoy all things. I got nothing that I asked for- but everything I had hoped for. Almost despite myself, my unspoken prayers were answered. I am among men, most richly blessed." — Found on the body of a dead Confederate soldier 1861-1865

Amazing the level of peace and joy that can be found only in the storm.

Simplicity

Simplicity is where the Clean Air Act is eventually headed. It is inevitable as Chesterton puts it.

-----"The whole world is certainly heading for a great simplicity, not deliberately, but rather inevitably.

The simplicity towards which the world is driving is the necessary outcome of all our systems and speculations and of our deep and continuous contemplation of things. For the universe is like everything in it; we have to look at it repeatedly and habitually before we see it. It is only when we have seen it for the hundredth time that we see it for the first time. The more consistently things are contemplated, the more they tend to unify themselves and therefore to simplify themselves. The simplification of anything is always sensational. [. . .]

Few people will dispute that all the typical movements of our time are upon this road towards simplification. Each system seeks to be more fundamental than the other; each seeks, in the literal sense, to undermine the other. In art, for example, the old conception of man, classic as the Apollo Belvedere, has first been attacked by the realist, who asserts that man, as a fact of natural history, is a creature with colourless hair and a freckled face. Then comes the Impressionist, going yet deeper, who asserts that to his physical eye, which alone is certain, man is a creature with purple hair and a grey face. Then comes the Symbolist, and says that to his soul, which alone is certain, man is a creature with green hair and a blue face. And all the great writers of our time represent in one form or another this attempt to reestablish communication with the elemental, or, as it is sometimes more roughly and fallaciously expressed, to return to nature. [. . .]
But the giants of our time are undoubtedly alike in that they approach by very different roads this conception of the return to simplicity. Ibsen returns to nature by the angular exterior of fact, Maeterlinck by the eternal tendencies of fable. Whitman returns to

nature by seeing how much he can accept, Tolstoy by seeing how much he can reject."— G.K. Chesterton

The Clean Air Act will eventually be simple. What a comforting hope in this inevitability.

Emphasis

You are far more important than what you are doing. And it is the outcome of the inner drama where ultimately rests the outer pageant of history.

The Wave

Life is short.

We are small.

We tend therefore to undertake only those things that we think we can be accomplish in this short life.

Three faults with this thinking:
1. Its time-blinded
2. It defines possibility only as what we can see
3. Places self as the end and scope of the endeavor

I won't elaborate on these points. I'll just share this story:

> "The Story is about a little wave, bobbing along in the ocean, having a grand old time. He's enjoying the wind and the fresh air—until he notices the other waves in front of him, crashing against the shore. "my god, this is terrible", the wave says. "Look what's going to happen to me!" Then along comes another wave. It sees the first wave, looking grim, and it says to him, "Why do you look so sad?" The first wave says, "You don't understand! We're all going to crash! All of us waves are going to be nothing! Isn't it terrible?" The second waves says, "No you don't understand, You're not a wave, you're part of the ocean."—Anonymous

Isaac Newton

I wonder what Isaac Newton would think about the Clean Air Act?

-----"I hate that each sector has 17 to 20 rules that govern each piece of equipment and you've got to be a neuroscientist to figure it out". --Gina McCarthy, U.S. EPA Administrator

> -----"Truth is ever to be found in the simplicity, and not in the multiplicity and confusion of things." ---Isaac Newton
> -----"Nature is pleased with simplicity. And nature is no dummy."---Isaac Newton
> -----"More is in vain when less will serve." ---Isaac Newton
> ----In the Principia, Newton simplified the explanation of what forces govern the movement of objects through the universe—distilling this immensely complex issue into just three basic laws.
> -----The idea of simplicity helped Newton to invent the reflecting telescope which was an alternative and a less complicated design to the refracting telescope which, at that time, was a design that suffered from severe chromatic aberration.
> -----"It is the perfection of God's works that they are all done with the greatest simplicity." --Isaac Newton

Shame and Remorse

I beat myself up a lot. Cling to the shame and remorse of past mistakes and omissions. Prideful to do this. Just pride that is suffering.

Seems like a lot of potential growth, whether it be to the Clean Air Act or to our personal lives, is stinted more by shame and remorse than by the underlying mistakes or omissions themselves.

Drop them. Unnecessary baggage. Hampering growth. The only thing dragging them around is pride.

-   "The pain you feel at your own imperfection is worse than the faults themselves." --Fenelon

-   "You would rather punish yourself, and stir up a commotion, than forget yourself and look to God. Mourning your weakness will not make you better. It will only contribute to a good case of self-pity. The slightest glance toward God will calm you far more."-- Fenelon

- "When we love truly, all oppression of past sin will be swept away."---George MacDonald

- "Your goal is to be as patient with yourself as you are with your neighbor."--Fenelon

- "Your old nature wants to be perfect. [. . .] Just be a little child."--Fenelon

- "For some are too proud to forgive themselves, till the forgiveness of God has had its way with them, has drowned their pride in the tears of repentance, and made their heart come again like the heart of a child."--George MacDonald

- "Shame is a thing to shame only those who want to appear, not those who want to be."--George MacDonald

Building a New Clean Air Act

How about working to build something new together? Here is an idea. If we succeeded in this endeavor we could greatly reduce costs to industry and the public--and improve environmental quality. There is a win-win future out there if we have the courage to seek it.

Imagine if a stationary source could be surrounded by some type of remote sensing or monitoring field that would measure air coming into and out of a facility. Imagine what this could mean? You would get real-world results (rather than relying on AP-42 factors and praying they are right in the field). You would have much more simplicity, transparency, and accountability. There would be no need for about 75% of the Clean Air Act and its regulations. Those regulations could and would need to be removed as explained below. A facility could do whatever it wanted within its bubble. You would not need NSR, Title V, MACT, BACT, or almost any other acronym. A facility could put in a 1955 boiler if it wants with no need for a permit, modification, BACT assessment, or the like. The only thing a facility could not do is exceed the limits of its bubble without ramifications. Imagine the billions of dollars that could be saved and real-world emissions that could be reduced? It would be revolutionary--essentially like the computer-age of air quality management.

We are almost there—and some would argue we are already there. One of the keys to this future is that industry cannot be required to calculate emissions with this new "computer" and also continue to be required to calculate emissions using a slide-rule and doing the calculations long-hand. We seem to have this tendency in environmental regulation to pile on requirements. We think that the more environmental regulations we add the better the environment will be. Not so. It's like a cup of black coffee. Just because we add more sugar doesn't mean that the coffee will keep tasting better. In fact at some point it will start tasting like crap. Remote sensing offers an opportunity to simplify. Remote sensing offers an opportunity to decrease both emissions as well as compliance costs. If what we end up with in the end though is only pushing more requirements on industry without removing unnecessary and duplicative requirements we will not succeed in accomplishing our ends. It is silly and a waste of business and government resources to do calculations both with a computer, a calculator, a slide-rule, and long-hand. Plus these results will differ—leading to conflicting standards. Also, as we all know, companies can move more operations overseas where there are less controls and it's cheaper to operate. More product might be produced overseas and arrive to the U.S. via ship. This would increase emissions. Moreover, some of the displaced emissions will reach us via the wind (e.g. long-range transport—it's happening). Finally, my brothers and sisters in Nigeria will be faced with breathing more pollution—and pollution for creating products intended for me. Why should I not care just as much about their children as I do my own?

Remote sensing offers a win-win opportunity—saving companies substantial amounts in compliance costs while improving environmental performance and keeping jobs here in America.

We must simplify our system. We have an opportunity to do so. With simplicity will come better transparency. With transparency will come better accountability. The more simple things are, the more everyone understands them. The more everyone understands them, the better they can comply with them. It's that simple.

> -----"*Progress lies not in enhancing what is, but in advancing toward what will be.*" - Kahlil Gibran

Beethoven's 9th Symphony

Still think we can't reform the Clean Air Act? Guess what. We already are. This is just the first movement. Want to hear what the final movement will sound like? Listen to the 4th movement of Beethoven's Ninth. My favorite part of the 4th movement is how dark it begins. And then out of this darkness comes the oboes with the first hint of the melody that we all know so well. Then the melody is cast out by the darkness of the basses. But only to be heard again. This time by the cellos. And then by other instruments. This back and forth continues throughout the 4th movement. Each time the sounds of darkness become shorter and more distant, while the sounds of light continue to crescendo— finally culminating and erupting in the choral finale:

> -----*Froh, wie seine Sonnen fliegen Durch das Himmels praecht'gen Plan, Laufet, Brueder, eure Bahn, Freudig wie ein Held zum Siegen.*
>
> *Gladly as His suns do fly Through the heavens' splendid plan, Run now, brothers, your own course, Joyful like a conquering hero*
>
> *Seid umschlungen, Millionen! Diesen Kuss der ganzen Welt! Brueder - ueberm Sternenzelt Muss ein lieber Vater wohnen.*
>
> *Embrace each other now, you millions! The kiss is for the whole wide world! Brothers - over the starry firmament A beloved Father must surely dwell.*
>
> *Ihr stuerzt nieder, Millionen? Ahnest du den Schoepfer, Welt? Such ihn ueberm Sternenzelt, Ueber Sternen muss er wohnen.*
>
> *Do you come crashing down, you millions? Do you sense the Creators presence, world? Seek Him above the starry firmament, For above the stars he surely dwells.*

And so it will be.

Moving Mountains

Complexity builds mountains. Simplicity moves mountains.

> -----"Simple can be harder than complex: You have to work hard to get your thinking clean to make it simple. But it's worth it in the end because once you get there, you can move mountains." —*Steve Jobs*

Time to simplify and transform the Clean Air Act to better prepare ourselves for the problems and opportunities of a 21st century world. We can make it happen.

Jumping out of the Trench—Clean Air Act Reform

When we look back at history we can see all the great opportunities previous generations had for demonstrating their courage and faith. Embarking on ships sailing for the "edge of the world". Jumping out of trenches and fox holes to fight the spread of fascism and the third reich. Scampering for food to feed their families and others in the dust bowl of the 1930's.

I think the next generation will look on our generation and see that most of our opportunities for courage and faith came while sitting around meeting rooms in clean white shirts and sharply pressed suits and dresses. How will we be viewed? Did we have the courage to jump out of the trench? Did we have the courage to leave the shore?

"It's not the right time"

Many people have said to me, "Clean Air Act transformation is clearly the right thing to do, but it just can't happen in the current political environment, and therefore, we are better off just figuring out how to make the best of our current situation." Below is my response.

> "The story of human progress has been written not by people asking "what is politically do-able" or "how can I do this and not get hurt", but by people who simply asked "what is the right thing to do"— trusting that all would be well if they only endeavored toward this one unfailing principle."--Jed Anderson

People throughout history have taken on much more significant problems, with far less resources, in far more turbulent times, with far more uncertainties, and with much greater peril to themselves. Thankfully Galileo and Susan B. Anthony didn't say, "well, I guess I can try to work within the current system". If the system works great. But if it doesn't work then it needs to be changed. It's that simple. It's not a big deal. Nothing to be afraid of—even if we need to make a fundamental change. I think

everyone would agree that in retrospect it's been a good thing that we no longer hold on to the central tenet that the sun travels around the earth.

Transforming the Clean Air Act will relatively be piece of cake. Only question on whether to proceed or not should be "is this the right thing to do". After that its only about courage and faith.

Schoenbrod Saying Clean Air Act is Now "Stupid"

Wasn't it a huge relief to hear someone of Schoenbrod's renown sum up what the Clean Air Act has become in such a succinct and honest word? What beautiful grammatical profundity.

My dad was an alcoholic. Dad was a Lutheran minister—and one of the most beautiful souls to walk this earth. But Dad and vodka had a relationship. For many years Dad tried to intellectualize and rationalize the problem. Things didn't change. Things changed when Dad finally reduced the problem to just one word, walked into a room full of people, and said: "Hi . . . My name is Peter and I'm an alcoholic." One word. Salve on an open wound. Dad began to heal.

As long as we intellectualize and rationalize the Clean Air Act, we are like that alcoholic saying, "Yeah, this isn't a perfect situation, but it could be worse." Relief will come when each of us reduces this problem to one word, stands up in public, and says, "yeah . . . this has gotten 'stupid'". One word. Salve on an open wound. The healing will begin.

All will be well. All is well.

The Wrong Path

Maybe we are wrong for trying to transform the Clean Air Act. Maybe history will reveal that our purpose did not resonate with the truth—and our nation's reliance on the current Act was the best approach to cleaning the air.

That will be just fine.

------"*Let a man do right, nor trouble himself about worthless opinion; the less he heeds tongues, the less difficult will he find it to love men. Let him comfort himself with the thought that the truth must out. He will not have to pass through eternity with the brand of ignorant or malicious judgment upon him. He shall find his peers and be judged of them. "But, thou who lookest for the justification of the light, art thou verily prepared for thyself to encounter such exposure as the general unveiling of things must bring? Art thou willing for the truth whatever it be? I nowise mean to ask, Have you a conscience so void of offence, have you a heart so pure and clean, that you fear no fullest exposure of what is in you to the gaze of men and angels?—as to God, he knows it all now! What I mean to ask is, Do you so love the truth and the right, that you welcome, or at least submit willingly to the idea of an exposure of what in you is yet unknown to yourself-an exposure that may redound to the glory of the truth by making you ashamed and humble? It may be, for instance, that you were wrong in regard to those, for the righting of whose wrongs to you, the great judgment of God is now by you waited for with desire: will you welcome any discovery, even if it work for the excuse of others, that will make you more true, by revealing what in you was false? Are you willing to be made glad that you were wrong when you thought others were wrong? If you can with such submission face the revelation of things hid, then you are of the truth, and need not be afraid; for, whatever comes, it will and can only make you more true and humble and pure. "*— George MacDonald

How Much Longer until the Clean Air Act is Transformed?

A friend yesterday asked how far along the path we are in transforming the Clean Air Act. I'm not sure. We are not at the summit, but we aren't at the bottom anymore either.

Anyone ever climbed a hill or mountain? As you approach from a distance you see how high it is and you ask yourself "do I really want to do this". You think how long it will take. Your body groans in anticipation. You even think about staying in your car . . . but you don't. You strap on your boots and begin to walk. You are no longer focused on the summit now, but on the path in front of you. Your vision narrows to the next rock that must be overcome. Every once in a while you stop for water and look up. You look

out at the view and see how far you've come. You try to look at the summit again, but this time you can't see it because you are too close to the mountain. Still you know it's there. Your eyes again turn to the path. As you climb your body begins to ache, but underlying the pain is a feeling of strength that grows with every step. You feel the anticipation of the summit and the joy of being.

So it is with the Clean Air Act transformation effort. Eventually we will get to the summit. Just a matter of focusing on the path in front of us and continuing to move our feet. What a wonderful journey it is.

Henry David Thoreau

I wonder what Thoreau would think about the Clean Air Act?

-----"I hate that each sector has 17 to 20 rules that govern each piece of equipment and you've got to be a neuroscientist to figure it out". --Gina McCarthy, U.S. EPA Administrator

> -----"Our life is frittered away by detail. Simplify, simplify." ---Henry David Thoreau
> -----"Simplicity, simplicity, simplicity! ---Henry David Thoreau
> -----"I do believe in simplicity. [. . .] When the mathematician would solve a difficult problem, he first frees the equation of all incumbrances, and reduces it to its simplest terms. So simplify the problem of life, distinguish the necessary and the real. Probe the earth to see where your main roots run." ---Henry David Thoreau
> -----"A lady once offered me a mat, but as I had no room to spare within the house, nor time to spare within or without to shake it, I declined it." ---Henry David Thoreau
> -----"Simplicity is the law of nature for men as well as for flowers." ---Henry David Thoreau

Making Mistakes

Anyone make mistakes? I do. All the time. Generally not a big deal to make a mistake. The bigger deal is to remain in a mistake. Mistakes are forgiven. Leave to continue in a mistake is not.

-----"No man is condemned for anything he has done; he is condemned for continuing to do wrong. He is condemned for not coming out of the darkness, for not coming to the light."—George MacDonald

Not the Right Time

"I'd love to tell the truth about what I think about the Clean Air Act process. But I can't. It's just not the right time for me to speak up."

I wish I had your confidence that I will be on this earth long enough for it to become the right time. I am promised many things—but time doesn't seem to be one of them.

-----"Life is short, but truth works far and lives long: let us speak the truth." —Arthur Schopenhauer

Bruce Lee

I wonder what Bruce Lee would think about the Clean Air Act?

-----"I hate that each sector has 17 to 20 rules that govern each piece of equipment and you've got to be a neuroscientist to figure it out". --Gina McCarthy, U.S. EPA Administrator

-----"In building a statue, a sculptor doesn't keep adding clay to his subject. Actually, he keeps chiselling away at the inessentials until the truth of its creation is revealed without obstructions."---Bruce Lee
-----"To me, the extraordinary aspect of martial arts lies in its simplicity. The easy way is also the right way, and martial arts is nothing at all special; the closer to the true way of martial arts, the less wastage of expression there is." ---Bruce Lee
-----"It is not a daily increase, but a daily decrease. The height of cultivation always runs to simplicity." ---Bruce Lee

Albert Einstein

I wonder what Einstein would think about the Clean Air Act?

-----"I hate that each sector has 17 to 20 rules that govern each piece of equipment and you've got to be a neuroscientist to figure it out". --Gina McCarthy, U.S. EPA Administrator

> -----"If you can't explain it to a six year old, you don't understand it yourself."- Albert Einstein
> -----"The definition of genius is taking the complex and making it simple." ---Albert Einstein
> -----"Out of clutter, find simplicity." ---Albert Einstein
> -----"Most of the fundamental ideas of science are essentially simple, and may, as a rule, be expressed in a language comprehensible to everyone." ---Albert Einstein
> -----"When the solution is simple, God is answering." ---Albert Einstein

Steve Jobs

I wonder what Steve Jobs would think about the Clean Air Act?

-----"I hate that each sector has 17 to 20 rules that govern each piece of equipment and you've got to be a neuroscientist to figure it out". --Gina McCarthy, U.S. EPA Administrator

> -----"Simplicity is the ultimate sophistication." ---Steve Jobs
> -----"When you first start off trying to solve a problem, the first solutions you come up with are very complex, and most people stop there. But if you keep going, and live with the problem and peel more layers of the onion off, you can often times arrive at some very elegant and simple solutions."---Steve Jobs
> -----"That's been one of my mantras - focus and simplicity. Simple can be harder than complex: You have to work hard to get your thinking clean to make it simple. But it's worth it in the end because once you get there, you can move mountains. ---Steve Jobs

The Pope and Climate Change

Pascal wrote a book called "Penses". I guess that's how you could best characterize the following, "Thoughts". Read or hit the delete button. Up to you. I just wrote it for reasons I'm not sure of (probably many of them selfish and paltry). As always, "take what you want and leave the rest".

Pope Week and Climate Change

The Pope's in town. Speaking to Congress on Thursday--in part about climate change.
The Pope and I agree on climate change.

In fact, I'm the first and only person in U.S. history who has re-written the Clean Air Act . . . and re-written the Act to include climate change.

That being said, I'm not sure why the institutional church is trying to break into the area of governmental environmental policy when they are already involved via the laity. Seems like they are trying to break into their own house.

      ---"Life and religion are one, or neither is anything."--George MacDonald

In a nutshell, what I think the Saints and theologians below are saying is: If the institutional church wants better plumbing, then tell the plumber more about Christ, not about how Christ would do plumbing. The benefit to this approach is that not only will the church get better plumbing this way (and it's in their expertise) . . . they'll get the plumber. The plumbing is finite. The plumber is eternal. Long after earth's institutions, problems, and the galaxies are a distant tale--the plumber has the potential to still be alive-- and alive with more life than they ever knew.

If the Pope or church writes a book on forgiveness I'll buy it. But if the Pope or church writes a book on plumbing--or in this case the Pope analyzing economic strategies for environmental problems such as "cap-and-trade" and "carbon taxes"--I'm not. Maybe the Pope is right that these market-based approaches are not appropriate, but I don't think this is his area of particular expertise. I think that's our role in the Body of Christ. I have to tell you, it baffles me when the church has the power of the Eternal yet sometimes seems to dump this power in favor of the tools and methods of the finite—swinging around policy tools and pointed sticks like the rest of us (my church was even involved in litigation over refinery flexible air permit rules). God cannot be defeated, but I think the church potentially can. And I think if it is defeated its demise will likely be because of its own accord it has given up the powers of the Eternal in favor of the tools of this earth, and has come down onto a level plane in which it fights like the rest of us and therefore can be defeated. My hope and prayer is that the church rests in the powers of the Eternal. As Napolean Bonaparte once said, "There

are only two forces in the world, the sword and the spirit. In the long run the sword will always be conquered by the spirit." The church knows the quickest and easiest path to solving all of our problems. Everything else will follow if they point us at this figure.

Just a couple more thoughts I wanted to share. I think C.S. Lewis was correct below when he pointed out the dangers to the church in becoming "Christianity And" (e.g. "Christianity and the Crisis, Christianity and the New Psychology, Christianity and Vegetarianism, Christianity and Spelling Reform). And I think Lewis was right when he pointed out how the purpose of the church can get "muddled" . . . and that the church suggesting to the laity how to implement a policy program is "silly" (see below). But even if you disagree with Lewis' assertion that society will come about more quickly by the church focusing Christians on religious matters rather than social matters, I hope you will agree with Temple's assertion that even if the Church's role is to "point out where the existing social order is in conflict with [Christian principles]", the church must then "pass on to Christian citizens, acting in their civic capacities, the task of reshaping the existing order in closer conformity to the principles." And the fact is that the Pope and the church are not passing. They are trying to do the work themselves when they delve into the merits of economic theories.

I hope each of us will see that we are the Church when it comes to implementing "do as you would want to be done by" into environmental policy approaches. And that there is no such thing as a sacred versus a secular approach. Everything is sacred. We are one Body made of many parts. Although the laity must be admonished, our role in the Body must be respected. And because we have a respected role as part of the Body, the Body is depending on us to fulfill our role. We must fulfill it. You and I can make it happen. All will be well. All is well.

C.S. Lewis Statement on the Role of the Institutional Church and the Laity

----- *"The second thing to get clear is that Christianity has not, and does not profess to have, a detailed political programme for applying "Do as you would be done by" to a particular society at a particular moment. It could not have. It is meant for all men at all times, and the particular programme which suited one place or time would not suit another. And, anyhow, that is not how Christianity works. When it tells you to feed the hungry it does not give you lessons in cookery. When it tells you to read the Scriptures it does not give you lessons in Hebrew and Greek, or even in English grammar. It was never intended to replace or supersede the ordinary human arts and sciences; it is*

rather a director which will set them all to the right jobs, and a source of energy which will give them all new life, if only they will put themselves at its disposal.

People say, "The Church ought to give us a lead." That is true if they mean it in the right way, but false if the mean it in the wrong way. By the Church they ought to mean the whole body of practicing Christians. And when they say that the Church should give us a lead, they ought to mean that some Christians--those who happen to have the right talents -- should be economists and statesmen, and that all economists and statesmen should be Christians, and that their whole efforts in politics and economics should be directed to putting "Do as you would be done by" in to action. If that happened, and if we others were really ready to take it, then we should find the Christian solution for our own social problems pretty quickly. But of course, when they ask for a lead from the Church most people mean they want the clergy to put out a political programme. That is silly. The clergy are those particular people within the whole Church who have been specially trained and set aside to look after what concerns us as creatures who are going to live forever; and we are asking them to do a quite different job for which have not been trained. The job is really on us, on the laymen. The application of Christian principles, say to trade unionism and education, must come from Christian trade unionists and Christian schoolmasters; just as Christian literature comes from Christian novelists and dramatists—not from the bench of bishops getting together and trying to write plays and novels in their spare time. [. . .]

A Christian society is not going to arrive until most of us really want it; and we are not going to want it until we become fully Christian. I may repeat 'Do as you would be done by' till I am black in the face, but I cannot really carry it out till I love my neighbor as myself: and I cannot love my neighbor as myself till I learn to love God: and I cannot learn to love God except by learning to obey Him. And so, as I warned you, we are driven on to something more inward -- driven on from social matters to religious matters. For the longest way round is the shortest way home." - C.S. Lewis, Mere Christianity

-----"My dear Wormwood: The real trouble about the set your patient is living in is that it is merely Christian. They all have individual interests, of course, but the bond remains mere Christianity. What we want, if men become Christians at all, is to keep them in the state of mind I call "Christianity And." You know—Christianity and the Crisis, Christianity and the New Psychology, Christianity and the <u>New Order</u>, Christianity and Faith Healing, Christianity and Psychical Research, Christianity and Vegetarianism, Christianity and Spelling Reform. If they must be Christians, let them at least be Christians with a difference. Substitute for the faith itself some Fashion with a Christian colouring. Work on their horror of the Same Old Thing." –C.S. Lewis

---- From many letters to "The Guardian" and from much that is printed elsewhere, we learn of the growing desire for a Christian `party', a Christian `front', or a Christian `platform' in politics. [. . .] It is not reasonable to suppose that such a Christian Party will acquire new powers of leavening the infidel organization to which it is attached.

*Why should it? Whatever it calls itself, it will represent, not Christendom, but a part of Christendom. The principle which divides it from its brethren and unites it to its political allies will not be theological. It will have no authority to speak for Christianity; it will have no more power than the political skill of its members gives it to control the behaviour of its unbelieving allies. But there will be a real, and most disastrous novelty. It will be not simply a part of Christendom, but a part claiming to be the whole. By the mere act of calling itself the Christian Party it implicitly accuses all Christians who do not join it of apostasy and betrayal. It will be exposed, in an aggravated degree, to that temptation which the Devil spares none of us at any time --- the temptation of claiming for our favourite opinions that kind and degree of certainty and authority which really belongs only to our Faith. The danger of mistaking our merely natural, though perhaps legitimate, enthusiasms for holy zeal, is always great. Can any more fatal expedient be devised for increasing it than that of dubbing a small band of Fascists, Communists, or Democrats `the Christian Party'? The demon inherent in every party is at all times ready enough to disguise himself as the Holy Ghost; the formation of a Christian Party means handing over to him the most efficient make-up we can find. And when once the disguise has succeeded, his commands will presently be taken to abrogate all moral laws and to justify whatever the unbelieving allies of the `Christian' Party wish to do. If ever Christian men can be brought to think treachery and murder the lawful means of establishing the regime they desire, and faked trials, religious persecution and organized hooliganism the lawful means of maintaining it, it will, surely, be by just such a process as this. The history of the late medieval pseudo-Crusaders, of the Covenanters, of the Orangemen, should be remembered. On those who add `Thus said the Lord' to their merely human utterances descends the doom of a conscience which seems clearer and clearer the more it is loaded with sin."---**C.S. Lewis**

------ *The method of the Church's impact upon society at large should be twofold. First, the Church must announce Christian principles and point out where the existing social order is in conflict with them. Second, it must then pass on to Christian citizens, acting in their civic capacities, the task of reshaping the existing order in closer conformity to the principles.*

At this point, technical knowledge and practical judgments will be required. For example, if a bridge is to be built, the Church may remind the engineer that it is his obligation to provide a safe bridge, but is not entitled to tell him how to build it or whether his design meets this requirement.

A particular theologian may also be a competent engineer, and in this case he may be entitled to make a judgment on its safety. But he may do so because he is a competent engineer, and not because he is a theologian. His theological skills have nothing whatsoever to do with it.—William Temple

----*"If they [non-believers] find a Christian mistaken in a field which they themselves know well and hear him maintaining his foolish opinions about our books, how are they going to believe those books in matters concerning the resurrection of the dead, the hope of eternal life, and the kingdom of heaven, when they think their pages are full*

of falsehoods and on facts which they themselves have learnt from experience and the light of reason?" ---St. Augustine

---*"And now there is one last point in the text of our parable which we must explore, for it contains a hidden but very important clue to its meaning. It does not say that we as Christians or that we as the church are like a seed or leaven. What it says is that the kingdom of God is both of these. The distinction is important. We have not been commanded to mobilize the moral and spiritual forces of Christendom and infiltrate the modern world, including its social order, its culture, and its technology—perhaps even with the express intent of giving this old and rather weary Europe a shot of moral vitamins and pep it up religiously. What is involved is something incomparably more simple than any such expansion of the Christian mind and spirit. This emerges, if at all, only incidentally, as a pure by-product of the real thing. And this real and simple thing consists in our doing nothing whatsoever except to let the Word of the Lord germinate, grow, and flourish within us. Or, to put it the other way round, simply that we grow into ever-deeper fellowship with Christ (1 Cor. 1:5:Eph. 4:13,15). But if Jesus is to grow large, I must grow smaller and ever less important. Jesus can win the world only with people who want him and therefore want nothing for themselves. If Christendom wants to gain its own life—if it wants to be a factor which the world will regard, which will set the masses going, and show up in the newspaper columns—then it will lose its life. And only the one who at the outset does not look outward at all, but is simply and solely intent on magnifying Jesus day by day in his own life, quite automatically becomes a herald and a conqueror of the world. He will possess the earth."—Helmutt Thielicke*

"In Ursin's Arithmetic, which was used in my school days, a reward was offered to anyone who could find a miscalculation in the book. I also promise a reward to anyone who can point out in these numerous books a single proposal for external change, or the slightest suggestion of such a proposal, or even anything that in the remotest way even for the most nearsighted person at the greatest distance could resemble an intimation of such a proposal or of a belief that the problem is lodged in externalities, that external change is what is needed, that external change is what will help us.

[. . .]

There is nothing about which I have greater misgivings than about all that even slightly tastes of this disastrous confusion of politics and Christianity, a confusion that can very easily bring about a new kind and mode of Church reformation, a reverse reformation that in the name of reformation puts something new and worse in place of something old and better, although it is still supposed to be an honest-to-goodness reformation, which is then celebrated by illuminating the entire city.

Christianity is inwardness, inward deepening. If at a given time the forms under which one has to live are not the most perfect, if they can be improved, in God's name do so. But essentially Christianity is inwardness. Just as man's advantage over animals is to be able to live in any climate, so also Christianity's perfection, simply because it is

inwardness, is to be able to live, according to its vigor, under the most imperfect conditions and forms, if such be the case. Politics is the external system, this Tantalus-like busyness about external change.

It is apparent from his latest work that Dr R. believes that Christianity and the Church are to be saved by 'the free institutions.' If this faith in the saving power of politically achieved free institutions belongs to true Christianity, then I am no Christian, or, even worse, I am a regular child of Satan, because, frankly, I am indeed suspicious of these politically achieved free institutions, especially of their saving, renewing power. . . . [I] have had nothing to do with 'Church' and 'state' – this is much too immense for me. Altogether different prophets are needed for this, or, quite simply, this task ought to be entrusted to those who are regularly appointed and trained for such things. I have not fought for the emancipation of 'the Church' any more than I have fought for the emancipation of Greenland, commerce, or women, of the Jews, or of anyone else."--Soren Kierkegaard

-----"The essence of the gospel does not lie in the solution of human problems, and the solution of human problems cannot be the essential task of the church." –Dietrich Bonhoeffer

-----"And this is the mission of the church—not civilization, but salvation—not better laws, purer legislation, social elevation, human equality, and liberty, but first, the "kingdom of God and His righteousness;" regenerated hearts, and all other things will follow. --A. E. Kittredge.

-----"THE TRULY WISE talk little about religion, and are not given to taking sides on doctrinal issues. When they hear people advocating or opposing the claims of this or that party in the church, they turn away with a smile such as men yield to the talk of children. They have no time, they would say for that kind of thing. They have enough to do in trying to faithfully practice what is beyond dispute." ----George McDonald

-----"What was perfect empire to the Son of God, while he might teach one human being to love his neighbor, and be good like his father! [. . .] Government, I repeat, was to him flat, stale, unprofitable."---George MacDonald

-----"Church or chapel is not the place for divine service. It is a place of prayer, a place of praise, a place to feed upon good things, a place to learn of God, as what place is not? [. . .] But the world in which you move, the place of your living and loving and labor, not the church you go to on your holiday, is the place of divine service."---George MacDonald

Abilities

I still find people that think they can't change the Clean Air Act.

-----"It is a denial of the divinity within us to doubt our potential and our possibilities." - James Faust

I understand if you don't want to change the Clean Air Act, but you can't say that you can't. You can't hold on to a cosmic impossibility. Your potential exists whether you want it to or not.

Should We Change the Clean Air Act?

— "I cannot say whether things will get better if we change; what I can say is they must change if they are to get better." – Georg C. Lichtenberg
— "All conservatism is based upon the idea that if you leave things alone you leave them as they are. But you do not. If you leave a thing alone you leave it to a torrent of change." – G. K. Chesterton
— "The dogmas of the quiet past are inadequate to the stormy present. The occasion is piled high with difficulty, and we must rise with the occasion. As our case is new, so we must think anew and act anew." – Abraham Lincoln
— "Change alone is eternal, perpetual, immortal." – Arthur Schopenhauer
— "If you have always done it that way, it is probably wrong." – Charles Kettering
— "I am not an advocate for frequent changes in laws and constitutions, but laws and institutions must go hand in hand with the progress of the human mind. As that becomes more developed, more enlightened, as new discoveries are made, new truths discovered and manners and opinions change, with the change of circumstances, institutions must advance also to keep pace with the times. We might as well require a man to wear still the coat which fitted him when a boy as civilized society to remain ever under the regimen of their barbarous ancestors." – Thomas Jefferson
— "Change does not necessarily assure progress, but progress implacably requires change." – Henry Steele Commager

How Nature Works

It is ironic that a system we have designed to protect nature strays so far from emulating nature.

>-----"I hate that each sector has 17 to 20 rules that govern each piece of equipment and you've got to be a neuroscientist to figure it out". --Gina McCarthy, U.S. EPA Administrator

>-----"Nature is pleased with simplicity. And nature is no dummy."
— Isaac Newton

Simplifying the Operating System

What would happen if we simplified the Clean Air Act operating system?

- "We've gone through the operating system and looked at everything and asked how can we simplify this and make it more powerful at the same time."---Steve Jobs
- "A good system shortens the road to the goal."---Orison Marden

Time to simplify and transform the Clean Air Act. We can make it happen.

Everything is Impossible without Trying

The reason Clean Air Act reform is so difficult is we haven't tried it.

Start climbing and the mountain becomes smaller. Eventually you find yourself at the top wondering how you got there.

Einstein's 3 Rules of Work and the Clean Air Act

How might Einstein approach the Clean Power Plan, New Ozone Standard, and other challenges we face under the Clean Air Act? Easy to find. Here are Einstein's 3 rules of work:

1. "Out of clutter, find simplicity.
2. From discord, find harmony.

3. In the middle of difficulty lies opportunity."—Albert Einstein (his three rules of work)

Anyone want to try applying his 3 rules to the Clean Air Act? Does anyone else feel almost giddy when they think about the environmental and economic opportunities that could be realized?
What an incredible world we live in. What an incredible journey we are on. All will be well.

The world is changing. We must change with it. Time to simplify and transform the Clean Air Act to better prepare ourselves for the problems and opportunities of a 21st century world. We can make it happen.

Predicting the Future of the Clean Air Act

How can we predict the future of the Clean Air Act?

—–"The best way to predict the future is to create it."—Abraham Lincoln

Peace in Environmental Protection

Takes little courage to throw rocks in a rock throwing world.

The truly courageous hold hands.

Harder to get a rock thrown at you when everyone is holding hands.

"Re-evaluating the Clean Air Act would be disastrous"

Many Republican and Democrat leaders think that reevaluating the Clean Air Act would prove "disastrous".

I've got a one-word response to this . . . Courage. Oftentimes what appears to be the most dangerous thing to do in the long run is the safest thing to do.

—-"In a battle, or in mountain climbing, there is often one thing which it takes a lot of pluck to do; but it is also, in the long run, the safest thing to do. If you funk it, you will find yourself, hours later, in far worse danger. The cowardly thing is also the most dangerous thing.— C.S. Lewis, Mere Christianity

—"Take the case of courage. No quality has ever so much addled the brains and tangled the definitions of merely rational sages. Courage is almost a contradiction in terms. It means a strong desire to live taking the form of a readiness to die. 'He that will lose his life, the same shall save it,' is not a piece of mysticism for saints and heroes. It is a piece of everyday advice for sailors or mountaineers. It might be printed in an Alpine guide or a drill book. This paradox is the whole principle of courage; even of quite earthly or brutal courage. A man cut off by the sea may save his life if we will risk it on the precipice.

He can only get away from death by continually stepping within an inch of it. A soldier surrounded by enemies, if he is to cut his way out, needs to combine a strong desire for living with a strange carelessness about dying. He must not merely cling to life, for then he will be a coward, and will not escape. He must not merely wait for death, for then he will be a suicide, and will not escape. He must seek his life in a spirit of furious indifference to it; he must desire life like water and yet drink death like wine. No philosopher, I fancy, has ever expressed this romantic riddle with adequate lucidity, and I certainly have not done so. But Christianity has done more: it has marked the limits of it in the awful graves of the suicide and the hero, showing the distance between him who dies for the sake of living and him who dies for the sake of dying."— G.K. Chesterton, Orthodoxy

All will be well.

Clean Air Act is based on science . . . and the aim of science is simplicity

- "The main purpose of science is simplicity and as we understand more things, everything is becoming simpler." – Edward Teller

- "I'll tell you what you need to be a great scientist. You don't have to be able understand very complicated things. It's just the opposite. You have to be able to see what looks like the most complicated thing in the world and, in a flash, find the underlying simplicity. That's what you need: a talent for simplicity."— *Mitchell Wilson*

- "Science may be described as the art of systematic over-simplification."— *Karl Popper*

- "[T]he grand aim of all science...is to cover the greatest possible number of empirical facts by logical deductions from the smallest possible number of hypotheses or axioms."—Albert Einstein

- "Simplicity does not precede complexity, but follows it."- Alan J. Perlis

The world is changing. We must change with it. Time to simplify and transform the Clean Air Act. We can make it happen.

Clean Air Act is Headed for Simplicity

People say that life was simpler 100 years ago.

No, life was more ignorant a 100 years ago.

Ignorance is not simplicity. As our understanding grows, we as humans keep arranging and simplifying things as Chesterton and the scientists below point out. It's our nature. It's just how it all works. Everything is headed for a "great simplicity" as Chesterton articulates. And so it will be with air quality management. What a comfort it is to realize this.

- "The whole world is certainly heading for a great simplicity, not deliberately, but rather inevitably.

The simplicity towards which the world is driving is the necessary outcome of all our systems and speculations and of our deep and continuous contemplation of things. For the universe is like everything

in it; we have to look at it repeatedly and habitually before we see it. It is only when we have seen it for the hundredth time that we see it for the first time. The more consistently things are contemplated, the more they tend to unify themselves and therefore to simplify themselves. The simplification of anything is always sensational. [. . .]

Few people will dispute that all the typical movements of our time are upon this road towards simplification. Each system seeks to be more fundamental than the other; each seeks, in the literal sense, to undermine the other. In art, for example, the old conception of man, classic as the Apollo Belvedere, has first been attacked by the realist, who asserts that man, as a fact of natural history, is a creature with colourless hair and a freckled face. Then comes the Impressionist, going yet deeper, who asserts that to his physical eye, which alone is certain, man is a creature with purple hair and a grey face. Then comes the Symbolist, and says that to his soul, which alone is certain, man is a creature with green hair and a blue face. And all the great writers of our time represent in one form or another this attempt to reestablish communication with the elemental, or, as it is sometimes more roughly and fallaciously expressed, to return to nature. [. . .]

But the giants of our time are undoubtedly alike in that they approach by very different roads this conception of the return to simplicity. Ibsen returns to nature by the angular exterior of fact, Maeterlinck by the eternal tendencies of fable. Whitman returns to nature by seeing how much he can accept, Tolstoy by seeing how much he can reject."— G.K. Chesterton

Suffering and the Clean Air Act

Sentiment: "I don't' want to suffer. I want the Clean Air Act to be transformed, but I don't want people to laugh at me, ignore me, or despise me. I understand this is to be expected, and that this is part of the process, but I don't want too suffer more. My life is already painful enough."

- "I want to suffer so that I may love."—Fyodor Dostoyevsky
- "Character cannot be developed in ease and quiet. Only through experience of trial and suffering can the soul be strengthened, ambition inspired, and success achieved."— Helen Keller

- "Suffering has been stronger than all other teaching, and has taught me to understand what your heart used to be. I have been bent and broken, but – I hope – into a better shape."— Charles Dickens
- "I think it is very good when people suffer. To me that is like the kiss of Jesus."— Mother Teresa
- "When it is all over you will not regret having suffered; rather you will regret having suffered so little, and suffered that little so badly."–St. Sebastian Valfre
- "Blessed be He, Who came into the world for no other purpose than to suffer."–St. Teresa of Avila
- "I do not desire to die soon, because in Heaven there is no suffering. I desire to live a long time because I yearn to suffer much for the love of my Spouse."–St. Mary Magdalene de Pazzi
- "Never to suffer would never to have been blessed."—- Edgar Allan Poe
- "You will be consoled according to the greatness of your sorrow and affliction; the greater the suffering, the greater will be the reward."–St. Mary Magdalen de'Pazzi
- "Suffering is a great favor. Remember that everything soon comes to an end . . . and take courage. Think of how our gain is eternal."–St. Teresa of Avila
- "The road is narrow. He who wishes to travel it more easily must cast off all things and use the cross as his cane. In other words, he must be truly resolved to suffer willingly for the love of God in all things."–St. John of the Cross
- "The truth that many people never understand, until it is too late, is that the more you try to avoid suffering the more you suffer because smaller and more insignificant things begin to torture you in proportion to your fear of being hurt."—Thomas Merton
- "All the science of the Saints is included in these two things: To do, and to suffer. And whoever had done these two things best, has made himself most saintly."–Saint Francis de Sales
- "Consider the life of Jesus. He was born in a stable. He had to flee to Egypt. He worked 30 years in the shop of a craftsman. He suffered hunger, thirst and fatigue. He was poor and He was ridiculed. He taught the doctrine of heaven and no one listened to him. He was treated like a slave, betrayed, and died between two thieves. Jesus' life was full of humiliation, but we are horrified by the slightest humiliation. How do you expect to know Jesus if you do not see Him where He was found: in suffering and the cross. You must imitate Him. But do not think you can follow Him in your own

strength – you are going to have to find all your strength in Him. Remember that Jesus wants to feel all your weaknesses."—Fenelon

I Re-Wrote the Clean Air Act

I re-wrote the Clean Air Act (see "Clean Air and Climate Change Act of 2015").

- "It always seems impossible until it's done." – Nelson Mandela

Definition of an Air Quality Plan under the Current Clean Air Act

"SIP": (n.) A State air plan that generally tells the Federal government what the Federal government is doing so that the Federal government can tell the States that they have properly told the Federal government what the Federal government is doing.

Must simplify the Clean Air Act. The world is changing. We must change with it. Time to transform the Clean Air Act. We can make it happen.

Christmas Story: "Yes Viriginia, there can be a new Clean Air Act"

Some people think our dreams of a new Clean Air Act are not based in reality. We are just dreaming. And our dream is unlikely to ever come true.

No, yes, and maybe.

We understand the realities. There is nothing like pushing at the rock to get a sense of the weight of the rock. I think we just choose to believe in fairy dust. We can't prove it exists–just like you can't prove that it doesn't exist. I think we just get a sense that it might be here. And if we are later proven wrong that's ok. We just like a world better thinking there might be fairy dust in it.

A GLOBAL AIR POLLUTION AGREEMENT

World leaders are talking about an international agreement on climate change. Why not talk about all global pollutants at the same time? Seems like it might be more efficient since all these pollutants are blowing around and interacting with each other. Why not develop one coordinated and holistic approach?

It's becoming a "small multi-pollutant world after all". Here is a suggested name for the new international agreement:

"The Accord on Global Air Pollution and the Environment" or ("AGAPE")

The world is changing. We must change with it. Time to transform the Clean Air Act. We can make it happen

Playing Small Ball with the Clean Air Act

We seem to be in the "dead ball era" of environmental legislation. And we are apparently content to keep playing "small ball" with the courts and the agency.

Love Babe Ruth. Love how he changed the game of baseball. I imagine his thinking was something like this:

"Why keep trying to hit for singles? These guys keep getting thrown out all the time. And it's too much work. I think I'll hit it over that fence over there. Why run when I can walk."

Time to stop with the small ball with the Clean Air Act. Time to try to hit one over the fence.

First Bike Ride and the Clean Air Act

BOY: "I CAN'T RIDE A BIKE."
DAD: "HAVE YOU TRIED?"
BOY: "NO. BUT I CAN'T. IT'S TOO HARD."
DAD: "SON . . . THE REASON WHY YOU CAN'T RIDE A BIKE IS BECAUSE YOU HAVEN'T TRIED. NOT EVEN LANCE ARMSTRONG CAN RIDE A BIKE IF HE DOESN'T TRY TO RIDE A BIKE. IT'S PHYSICALLY IMPOSSIBLE. JUST TRY TO RIDE IT. THE RESULT MIGHT SURPRISE YOU."

Think about it. The main reason we haven't modernized the Clean Air Act is not because it's too hard. It's because we haven't tried.

Time to try.

Refreshingly Honest Comments About the Clean Air Act

Refreshingly honest quotes about the current state of the Clean Air Act after the U.S. Supreme Court's recent ruling in *Homer City*:

—-"The Court helped out a stupid statute, but we still have a stupid statute."—David Schoenbrod
—-"The Court really had to 'shoehorn' this result into this antique statute."—David Schoenbrod
—-"The Clean Air Act as it was enacted in 1970 is no good whatsoever with dealing with pollutants that go across State lines."—David Schoenbrod
—-"It [the Clean Air Act] was designed with the thought in mind that most pollution that we breathe in comes from sources in our State. Therefore, Congress could tell the States to clean up their acts and everything would be fine. The problem is today the vast bulk of pollution comes from many, many hundreds, if not thousands of miles away, so it's really a national problem. So it's kind of nuts to have the Federal Government telling the States to regulate pollution."—David Schoenbrod
—-"We ought to be able to go further, but we can't because the statute is stupid."—David Schoenbrod

The world is changing. We must change with it. Time to transform the Clean Air Act. We can make it happen.

The Story of How the Clean Air Act was Opened

Linda walked up to a door. On the door were written the words, "Clean Air Act". Linda tried to open the door. But the door was locked.

Nathan arrived at the door. Seeing Linda standing there, Nathan asked, "Is the door locked?". Linda replied, "Yes!". . . "Oh," Nathan dejectedly replied—deciding not to try the door for himself based on what he had been told.

Steven then showed up. Assuming that Linda and Nathan wouldn't be standing there if the door was open—Steven didn't even ask if the door was unlocked, but just took a position at the back of the line.

Years went by. Hundreds of people arrived. At some point the door was unlocked from the inside, but no one heard the latch being turned over the din of discussion that arose on how to get into the room without opening the door. Each person arriving at the door just assumed that the door was locked, and that if the crowd hadn't opened the door, they wouldn't be able to open the door either.

Finally Mary arrived. Pressing her way through the crowd Mary asked, "Hey, has anyone tried to open the door in a while?" Mary then knocked three times, turned the knob, . . . and walked through the doorway.

Running and the Clean Air Act

How can we keep running toward the goal of a more simplified Clean Air Act?

Don't make the end our joy.

Anyone else like running? Doesn't matter if there is a finish line does it? It's the freedom and joy of the body in motion. It's the straining of the muscles

and feel of the path underfoot that fills us with life. In our heart of hearts we would prefer if there were no finish lines. Finish lines say stop. We just want to run.

Fear and the Clean Air Act

The main reason most people don't want to change the Clean Air Act is because they're scared.
People on the left and right are afraid if the Clean Air Act's opened . . . the other side's gonna win.

A simple antidote to fear. Courage. And it's easily obtained. All we need to do is ask for it.

> *Fear knocked at the door.*
> *Faith answered.*
> *There was no one there.*
> *–Unknown*

All will be well.

Secret to Genius and Improving the Clean Air Act

The secret to genius is not intelligence. It's simplicity. And we are all capable of it. Mainly requires courage.

> - "Any intelligent fool can make things bigger, more complex, and more violent. It takes a touch of genius—and **a** lot of courage—to move in the opposite direction."—E.F. Schumacher (1911 – 1977)

Time to simplify the Clean Air Act. New measurement tools are available that can help us do this. We can make it happen.

Energy and the Clean Air Act

Important to remember that one day all these climate change and air quality regulatory arguments will largely be moot. It won't be tomorrow . . . but it will be some tomorrow.

Most of the world's air pollution is related to energy use and production. Energy just keeps getting cleaner, more efficient, and more abundant. It has to (see Richard Smalley's *"The Terrawatt Challenge"*). An inevitability that most of the Clean Air Act therefore eventually won't be needed. Isn't this wonderful!

What a great future we are headed toward!
- "Progress lies not in enhancing what is, but in advancing toward what will be."—Kahlil Gibran

Most Overlooked Way to Improve Air Quality

Probably the easiest and most overlooked way to improve air quality in the U.S. is to simplify the Clean Air Act.

- "The more you explain it, the more I don't understand it."-**Mark Twain**

Time to simplify the Clean Air Act. We can make it happen.

How can Foreign Pollution Blow into the U.S. without Blowing into a State?

Amazing that EPA Administrator Gina McCarthy, NASA, NOAA, EPA, the United Nations, the National Academy of Sciences, Harvard University, Princeton University, UC Davis, Columbia University, etc. are all saying that ozone-related pollution is blowing into the U.S. from overseas—yet not even one State recognizes this.

Don't take my word for it. Look for yourself. I am not aware of even one ozone plan in the whole U.S. that expressly recognizes that even a molecule of overseas industrial pollution blows into a State.

This raises the question:

- How can foreign pollution blow into the United States without blowing into a State?

This is the assumption we are making.

The problem of course is that if a State acknowledges foreign pollution impacts they will thereby acknowledge that the State has been unknowingly or knowingly requiring local citizens to offset this foreign pollution with additional controls on local sources in order to demonstrate attainment of the NAAQS.

I know that accepting new truths is painful—but living in untruths is even more painful. I bet everyone of us in our personal lives have come to this realization.

-----"Truth, like surgery, may hurt, but it cures." —Hans Suyin

The Horse Trade

Update the Clean Air Act. Needs to be updated anyway. Been 23 years. Already been revised 4 times. Inevitable it happens again. Might as well be now. Here is the proposed horse trade:

▶ **Democrats:** You get climate change incorporated expressly in a statute and can avoid years of litigation. You also get a more simplified, transparent, and more effective Clean Air Act.

▶ **Republicans:** You get a more coordinated, more predictable, and less expensive regulatory system for all pollutants that essentially removes the permitting process and allows businesses to react quicker to market opportunities.

Sure seems better to horse trade than keep shoveling what comes out the back end.

Pushing at the Rock

People have told me that Clean Air Act transformation will never happen. It's politically impossible. I am wasting my time.

For whatever reason, sometimes it feels like you just gotta go push at the rock.

God indicated to a man that he had work for him to do, and showed him a large rock in front of his cabin. The Lord explained that the man was to push against the rock with all his might.

So, this the man did, day after day. For many years he toiled from sun up to sun down; his shoulders set squarely against the cold, massive surface of the unmoving rock, pushing with all of his might. Each night the man returned to his cabin sore and worn out, feeling that his whole day had been spent in vain.

Since the man was showing discouragement, the Adversary (Satan) decided to enter the picture by placing thoughts into the weary mind: "you have been pushing against that rock for a long time, and it hasn't moved." Thus, giving the man the impression that the task was impossible and that he was a failure. These thoughts discouraged and disheartened the man.
Satan said, "Why kill yourself over this?" "Just put in your time, giving just the minimum effort; and that will be good enough." That's what he planned to do, but decided to make it a matter of prayer and take his troubled thoughts to the Lord.

"Lord," he said, "I have labored long and hard in your service, putting all my strength to do that which you have asked. Yet, after all this time, I have not even budged that rock by half a millimeter. What is wrong? Why am I failing?"

The Lord responded compassionately, "My friend, when I asked you to serve Me and you accepted, I told you that your task was to push against the rock with all of your strength, which you have done. Never once did I mention to you that I expected you to move it. Your task was to push.

And now you come to Me with your strength spent, thinking that you have failed. But, is that really so? Look at yourself. Your arms are strong and muscled, your back sinewy and brown, your hands are callused from constant pressure, your legs have become massive and hard. Through opposition you have grown much, and your abilities now surpass that which you used to have. Yet you haven't moved the rock. But your calling was to be obedient and to push

and to exercise your faith and trust in My wisdom. This you have done. Now I, my friend, will move the rock.

Clean Air Act vs. Simplicity

Compare the following quotes on simplicity vs. the Clean Air Act:

Clean Air Act
- "I hate that each sector has 17 to 20 rules that govern each piece of equipment and you've got to be a neuroscientist to figure it out". –Gina McCarthy, U.S. EPA Administrator
- "The Clean Air Act is a model of redundancy. Virtually every type of pollutant is regulated by not one but several overlapping provisions." – Ben Lieberman
- "The Clean Air Act is a lengthy and complex federal law" – Florida Department of Environmental Protection
- "The federal Clean Air Act (CAA) alone has been referred to as the most complicated statute in history. The statutory complexity is compounded by the thousands of pages of federal regulations and the overlapping statutes and regulations adopted by each individual state." –Erich Brich writing for the American Bar Association
- "The Clean Air Act – one of the most complex and extensive pieces of federal environmental legislation." –Center on Congress—Indiana University
- "The Clean Air Act is complicated and contentious". —Senate Environment and Public Works Committee
- "The Clean Air Act (CAA) is a comprehensive and complex piece of environmental legislation". – NASDA
- "The law is long and complicated". —Andrew Restuccia
- "The statute and its regulatory offshoots are very complicated." —U.S. Department of Justice

Simplicity
- "The ability to simplify means to eliminate the unnecessary so that the necessary may speak." —-Hans Hofmann
- "Our life is frittered away by detail. Simplify, simplify." —Henry David Thoreau
- "There is no greatness where there is not simplicity, goodness, and truth." — Leo Tolstoy

- "Truth is ever to be found in the simplicity, and not in the multiplicity and confusion of things." – Isaac Newton
- "The simplest things are often the truest." — Richard Bach

Complexity and the Clean Air Act

—-"I hate that each sector has 17 to 20 rules that govern each piece of equipment and you've got to be a neuroscientist to figure it out". — **Gina McCarthy, U.S. EPA Administrator**

And here's what's even more interesting about this quote. I don't think a neuroscientist would even try to figure out this complicated system. A neuroscientist, being a scientist, would first simplify the system and ask what the complexity adds to understanding or solving a problem before trying to understand it's complexity. Take for example the laws of accelerated motion:

$$S = a + ut + \tfrac{1}{2}gt^2 + bt^3$$

Neither Galileo nor any student of physics would consider using a higher degree polynomial in calculating the horizontal distance of an object falling from an inclined plane. You might wonder, "a higher degree polynomial would increase accuracy—so why would scientists prefer the simpler quadratic equation?" Because adding the higher degree polynomial makes it unnecessarily complicated without significantly improving the law. And crazy as this might initially sound, the higher degree polynomial actually is likely to yield much larger errors than the simpler quadratic law because of the wider oscillation in increasing data points.

Time to use the scientific method on the Clean Air Act. Time to simplify the Act so we can better understand the law and reduce the chance of error. We can make it happen.

Marriage and the Clean Air Act

The U.S. Supreme Court heard oral arguments today on the cross-state air pollution rule. Governors from the Eastern States also have filed a petition with EPA seeking additional emission reductions from the Midwestern States.

Let's see . . . the Northeastern States are pointing fingers at the Midwestern States. The Midwestern States are pointing fingers at the Western States. And the Western States are pointing fingers at the Far East.

Lots of finger pointing.

Does finger-pointing work for anyone? Anyone's marriage improving because of it? It's not helping mine. Finger-pointing just seems to suck up my time, emotions, and resources from working on myself—which is the only thing I can control and which is my only real access point to improving my marriage.

Maybe we should develop an air quality management system that doesn't require all this finger-pointing and requires us just to focus on ourselves? Seems like both marriages and Clean Air Acts work better when everyone is focused on what they can do to improve to the situation.

The world is changing. We must change with it. Time to transform the Clean Air Act. We can make it happen.

Human History and the Clean Air Act

Think about the length of human history. Now think about the Clean Air Act. It's a dot. One day the dot will be gone. It's just a fact. As they say, "History repeats itself . . . and that's one of the things wrong with history". We are often time-blinded and give undue weight to the present circumstances and the institutions around us that appear immovable—not seeing the finiteness of the moment and the infinity in which we are engulfed. The effect can be paralyzing. One way to regain perspective is to remember that historical events come and go, that you will outlive the Clean Air Act, and that the people you see each day at the bus stop or grocery store carry far more power than institutions such as the Clean Air Act.

- "There are no ordinary people. You have never talked to a mere mortal. Nations, cultures, arts, civilizations, [the Clean Air Act]– these are mortal, and their life is to ours as the life of a gnat. But it is immortals whom we joke with, work with, marry, snub and exploit. ... Next to the Blessed Sacrament itself, your neighbor is the holiest object presented to your senses." — C.S. Lewis, *The Weight of Glory*

Just some perspective that I find helpful when thinking about the Clean Air Act. Perhaps you will find it helpful as well.

The world is changing. We must change with it. Time to transform the Clean Air Act. We can make it happen.

Guilt and the Clean Air Act

Anyone feel guilty for taking people's money to do a bunch of this unnecessarily complicated and procedurally laden work under the current Clean Air Act?

I've made hundreds of thousands of dollars for example just performing common control analyses and netting exercises. I'm happy to help clients with these issues—but part of me feels guilty for taking people's money to perform what I know has become unnecessarily complicated—and then turning around and trying to convince my conscience . . . "Well . . . that's just the way the system works".

Hair cutting seems to be an honest profession. You give someone a haircut—100% of what you earned was necessary to perform.

I'm not sure if I'm at 25%.

Three responses. One is to keep taking people's money and keep your mouth shut. Second is to remain in the system but open your mouth. Third is to become a hair stylist.

The world is changing. We must change with it. Time to transform the Clean Air Act. We can make it happen.

It's easy! . . . How to Reduce Litigation under the Clean Air Act

One of the central focuses of the Congressional Clean Air Act Forums so far has been the crazy amount of litigation on air quality matters. At one point the question came up about what we could do to reduce litigation. The room was silent.

Here is the answer.

You can't stop litigation from occurring, but you can significantly reduce the number of circumstances that lead to litigation. It's quite simple. It's just like arguments with our significant others. We can't stop arguments from happening. But we can significantly reduce the number of circumstances that lead to arguments. I for example can take the garbage out next time without being asked. I can elect not to tell an embarrassing story at our next dinner party.

Exact same strategy with air quality litigation. Right now you can sue on where the NAAQS are set, what nonattainment designations are made, all the various parts of the SIP, the underlying control measures in the SIP, the Federal approval of the control measures that should be in the SIP, the Federal approval of the State control measures in the SIP, the State re-approval of the Federal disapproval of the State control measures in the SIP, the Federal approval of the State-reapproval of the Federal disapproval of the control measures in the SIP, etc. Just need to reduce the number of opportunities for litigation and the litigation will decrease. It's that easy.

Anyone re-reviewed the recommendations in "Breaking the Logjam" (see attached)? If not, I would encourage you to look at it again. Just think about the decreases in potential litigation this simplified air quality management process would provide versus our current paradigm. A significant portion of the recommendation is a Federal multi-pollutant market based system. Lawyers by the way hate programs like the Acid Rain Program. Why? Too simple. Not enough complexity, ambiguity, and steps in the process to argue over.

- *"Any intelligent fool can make things bigger, more complex, and more violent. It takes a touch of genius — and a lot of courage — to move in the opposite direction."* ——E.F Schumacher

-

Time to reduce the number of opportunities for time-consuming and resource-intensive litigation. Time to transform the SIP process. We can make it happen.

We've Got No Power, No Money . . . I like our Chances!

Let's see. We've got no money. No power. And we are trying to change the Clean Air Act. I like our chances!

What? How can I like our chances? Because when the weak charge headlong into a challenge, acknowledging their weakness, and doing so in an manner that does not conform to the norms around them, they usually win. The political scientist Ivan Arreguín-Toft recently looked at every war fought in the past two hundred years between the strong and the weak. He looked at conflicts in which one side had at least ten times more power. The Goliaths of the world, he found, won in 71.5 per cent of the cases. Almost 1/3 of the time, however, the underdogs prevailed—which is significant in and of itself. Next Arreguín-Toft asked what happened when the underdogs though acknowledged their weakness and chose an unconventional strategy—like David dropping the armor his brothers had put on him, grabbing 5 smooth stones, and running at the giant. When Arreguín-Toft re-analyzed the data in search of an answer to this question, he found that the underdog's winning percentage went from 28.5% to 63.6%. Arreguín-Toft concluded that when underdogs choose not to play by Goliath's rules . . . they usually win—"even when everything we think we know about power says they shouldn't".

Time to transform the Clean Air Act. We've got no money. We've got no power. Just a bit of logic, love, and a willingness to run at the giant. I'm liking our chances!

Sleeping on the Couch

The Clean Air Act requires States to be responsible for pollution above their State or prove it's someone else's (CAA §§ 109a, 110, 126, 179B, 319(b)). How about instead we just require States to be responsible for pollution they cause and can control—like Canada is now doing?

Anyone married? Anyone have any luck pointing fingers at each other? Never seems to work for me.

Finger-pointing over pollutant transport seems to just temporarily re-arrange the furniture and increase the chances of sleeping on the couch.

Time to transform the Clean Air Act. Time to focus our efforts on what is in our power to control. We can make it happen.

Path to Finding the Truth

How do we each seek the truth as best we can about the Clean Air Act? Like seeking the truth in anything, I think it first begins with a removal of self. You might ask, what? . . . Isn't this supposed to be about the Clean Air Act? Well yes, but I don't know if I would be being completely forthright with you if I only shared analytical reasoning about the Clean Air Act and didn't share with you what I believe lays at the core of discovering the truth about it. You see, I think there is an underlying current of truth and love that each of us share in common with each other—and the only way to find this commonality is to go beyond self. You might ask, who wants to lose themselves? Well, at their core I believe everyone does. I think we have been designed such that the more we lose ourselves and our self-will—the happier, the more joyful, and the more at peace we get. This is not easy, but I think this is what we so desperately desire. And to begin to find the truth in anything I think this must be our starting place.

I got an email several years ago from someone who wanted off this distribution list. The reason he wanted off was that although he appreciated the legal and policy analysis about the Clean Air Act, he did not appreciate the interjections about truth and love. If I thought the Clean Air Act problem was simply an analytical problem, or that we were simply finite creatures being guided only by the limits of our own analytical minds, then I think that interjecting thoughts of truth and love into this discussion would be superfluous and unwarranted. But I don't think this is the case. Truth and love seem to be at the core. To be reminded of this, to summon this, so that all the tools of our being can be brought to bear on our problems doesn't seem like it could be a bad thing. And frankly I'm not sure I could stuff them even if I wanted to.

At the end of the day I'm not sure what the truth will be about the Clean Air Act. What I do know though is that the only way to find truth is to seek it, and the more that self is removed the easier this seeking becomes.

> -----"From within or from behind, a light shines through us upon things, and makes us aware that we are nothing, but the light is all."
> -----Emerson

All will be well.

Finger-pointing and the Clean Air Act

The goal now seems to be what State can do the best finger-pointing (see article below). "It wasn't my pollution . . . it was hers!"

When my kids point fingers at each other after I ask them who threw the grape from the back of the mini-van I tell them, "I don't care who threw it . . . stop it and take responsibility for your own actions." We can't use this approach however when it comes to cleaning the air. Unfortunately, we have a law that requires States to not only take responsibility for their own actions—but to prove that their brother threw the grape.

State's should not need to spend their time and resources proving the trajectory of the grape, the mass of the grape, the location of where their siblings were seated, and the propensity of a given sibling to throwing things.

Time to align responsibility and authority. Time to transform the Clean Air Act so we don't need to spend our time and resources finger-pointing. We can make it happen.

Most Frequent Excuse for not Changing the Clean Air Act

Probably the most frequent excuse I hear for not wanting to try to improve the Clean Air Act is if we give this thing to Congress you never know what they will do with it. I imagine George Washington was thinking the same thing when he thought about keeping his powers to himself after the war of independence. His first thought had to have been to look over at Congress and think to himself, "Look at all these yahoos". Fortunately, Washington replied, "I didn¹t fight George III to become George I."

Democracy is a messy business. Churchill said, "Democracy is the worst form of government—except for all the others". The fact is the Clean Air Act is changing right now. And it's being changed by people with just as many side-agendas and who are just as imperfect as those in Congress (e.g. attorneys like me, judges, industry groups, non-profits, agency personnel, consultants, etc.).

We can have all kinds of excuses for not improving the Clean Air Act, but the one excuse we cannot have is that we don't trust Congress. To say that we are saying that we do not trust an elected form of government. Not an option.

Courage and Love

I wish I could tell everyone the stories of courage I've seen from several of you lately who have walked down that dark road holding a flash light. It hurts me to see the world not embracing you, but that is how we are told it is supposed to work. Know that. And keep loving the world even if it doesn't love you. Not only are we told that's what we are supposed to do, but apparently that's the key to feeling loved ourselves.

All the best to each of you on your journeys.

A Multi-Pollutant Approach

Let's see. We've got interrelated problems with interrelated solutions—all of which sometimes overlap and conflict. Yet despite these interrelationships, overlaps, and conflicts—we continue to follow an air quality planning process that consists of looking at each of these pollutant problems separately in relative isolation to one another. It's like we are building a place to live by building a bathroom, a bedroom, a family room, and a kitchen. Perhaps we could attach these rooms together to make the rooms more convenient to use and more efficient to heat? Perhaps it would take less building material if each of the rooms did not have its own roof, siding, and air conditioning system? Perhaps there might be benefits to considering if these rooms could be built together in one energy-efficient house?

The current Clean Air act is not designed to efficiently and effectively support a multi-pollutant approach. Foundational improvements are needed so that whatever is built is built on rock and not on sand.

Time to transform the Clean Air Act into a comprehensive multi-pollutant planning process that coordinates, prioritizes, and pursues reduction efforts

in the most efficient way possible considering various air quality and climate change goals. We can make it happen.

New EPA Rule

Everyone review EPA's proposed 8-hour ozone implementation rule. Commendable and admirable. I am reminded however of the following C.S. Lewis quote:

- "We all want progress, but if you're on the wrong road, progress means doing an about-turn and walking back to the right road; in that case, the man who turns back soonest is the most progressive." – – – -C.S. Lewis
-

I know your defense to this statement EPA is that you do not have the power to revise the Clean Air Act. I understand. But if you keep putting bondo on the 1990 Chevy Caprice and telling everyone how wonderful it is—it's going to take that much longer before we get a Prius or Tesla S.

The world is changing. We must change with it. Time to transform the Clean Air Act. We can make it happen.

Winston Churchill

I wonder what Churchill would think about the Clean Air Act?

-----"All the great things are simple." ---Winston Churchill
-----"If you have 10,000 regulations you destroy all respect for the law." ---Winston Churchill
-----"Out of intense complexities, intense simplicities emerge." --Winston Churchill

Time to transform the Clean Air Act. We can make it happen

Mother Pollard

When Martin Luther King asked an elderly woman affectionately known as Mother Pollard about how she was doing after days walking miles to town

during the Montgomery Bus Boycott she verbally smiled in true grammatical profundity:

---"My feets is tired, but my soul is rested."

I wish the same blessing for each of you in whatever journey you are on. May your feets be tired . . . and your soul rested.

Must Succeed

"We must succeed."

No . . . we must try.

-----"For us, there is only the trying. The rest is not our business."---T.S. Eliot

Cows and the Clean Air Act

I'm still laughing at the fact that this 5th Circuit Judge unknowingly and colloquially captured in one sentence what I've tried to say knowingly and intellectually in a thousand:

----*The Clean Air Act: "You gotta get it down to where the cows can get to it."*

Probably the best mantra for Clean Air Act reform I've ever heard.

Clean Air Act, Problems, and Laughter

Before self-criticism should come self-laughter. Laughter removes the exaggerated weight we give to our problems--freeing us to deal with the root of the problem rather than being trapped at the emotional surface of the problem. Not many big deals in this life. Laugh and look below the surface. All will be well.

- "Against the assault of laughter, nothing can stand." — Mark Twain

- "When we can begin to take our failures non-seriously, it means we are ceasing to be afraid of them. It is of immense importance to learn to laugh at ourselves." — Katherine Mansfield
- "At the height of laughter, the universe is flung into a kaleidoscope of new possibilities." — Jean Houston
- "To truly laugh, you must be able to take your pain and play with it." — Charlie Chaplin
- "To laugh at yourself is to love yourself."--Mickey Mouse
- "God is a comedian playing to an audience too afraid to laugh." — Voltaire
- "Laugh at yourself and at life. Not in the spirit of derision or whining self-pity, but as a remedy, a miracle drug, that will ease your pain, cure your depression, and help you put in perspective that seemingly terrible defeat and worry with laughter at your predicaments, thus freeing your mind to think clearly toward the solution that is certain to come. Never take yourself too seriously.-- Og Mandino
- "With the fearful strain that is on me night and day, if I did not laugh I should die."--Abraham Lincoln
- "To make mistakes is human; to stumble is commonplace; to be able to laugh at yourself is maturity."--William Arthur Ward
- "What is funny about us is precisely that we take ourselves too seriously." — Reinhold Neibuh

"I'm Tired"

Sentiment: "I'm tired of trying. These efforts are going nowhere. No one wants a better Clean Air Act. That's it. I'm done with this."

- "Our greatest weakness lies in giving up. The most certain way to succeed is to always try just one more time." ~ Thomas Edison
- "Success is stumbling from failure to failure with no loss of enthusiasm." — Winston S. Churchill
- "Energy and persistence alter all things."--Benjamin Franklin
- "If you have an important point to make, don't try to be subtle or clever. Use a pile driver. Hit the point once. Then come back and hit it again. Then hit it a third time - a tremendous whack." — Winston S. Churchill

- "Character consists of what you do on the third and fourth tries."— James A. Michener
- "Nothing in this world can take the place of persistence. Talent will not; nothing is more common than unsuccessful men with talent. Genius will not; unrewarded genius is almost a proverb. Education will not; the world is full of educated derelicts. Persistence and determination alone are omnipotent. The slogan Press On! has solved and always will solve the problems of the human race." — Calvin Coolidge
- "You may encounter many defeats, but you must not be defeated. In fact, it may be necessary to encounter the defeats, so you can know who you are, what you can rise from, how you can still come out of it." --Maya Angelou
- "To persist with a goal, you must treasure the dream more than the costs of sacrifice to attain it." ~ Richelle E. Goodrich
- "Permanence, perseverance, and persistence in spite of all obstacles, discouragement, and impossibilities: It is this, that in all things distinguishes the strong soul from the weak." ~ Thomas Carlyle
- "With ordinary talent and extraordinary perseverance, all things are attainable." ~Thomas Foxwell Buxton
- "It's not that I'm so smart, it's just that I stay with problems longer." ~ Albert Einstein
- "I'm a great believer in luck, and I find the harder I work, the more I have of it." ~Thomas Jefferson
- "All right Mister, let me tell you what winning means... you're willing to go longer, work harder, give more than anyone else." ~ Vincent Lombardi
- "Most people never run far enough on their first wind to find out they've got a second." ~ William James
- "Paralyze resistance with persistence." ~ Woody Hayes
- "Consider the postage stamp: Its usefulness consists in the ability to stick to one thing till it gets there." ~ Josh Billings
- "Courage and perseverance have a magical talisman, before which difficulties disappear and obstacles vanish into air."---John Quincy Adams
- "Let me tell you the secret that has led to my goal. My strength lies solely in my tenacity."---Louis Pasteur

Trying

Congress thinks they can't reform the Clean Air Act.

My kids tell me all the time they are unable to do things. Before I will believe them though, or want to help them, they need to answer the following question first:

❖ Have you tried?

Need to try. I still might not believe you can't do it if you try, but I refuse to believe you if you won't. There's a 100% chance of not succeeding without trying. And here's a strange truth that I tell my kids: People are much more prone to help if you try. It's just a weird truth about how the world works. If you try and really want something . . . "all the universe conspires in helping you to achieve it."--Paulo Coelho, The Alchemist

Weakness

"I feel weak."

Excellent.

Possible can be done under our own strength. Impossible requires weakness.

- *"When you feel absolutely weak you will discover a strength that is not your own."--Fenelon*

- *"Strength is made perfect in weakness. You are only strong in God when you are weak in yourself. Your weakness will be your strength if you accept it with a lowly heart."—Fenelon*

- *"How strong you will be when you see that you are completely weak."--Fenelon*

- *"The great profit to be derived from an experience of our weakness, is to render us lowly and obedient."—Fenelon*

Mom

Mom died a few months ago. This morning I read a journal she wrote for me before she died. The cover page reads, "To Jed: Love, Mom". I haven't been able to read it until now. Too painful. But for whatever reason I did this morning. Glad I did. It was sunshine.

A few quips from Mom that seemed pertinent to our Clean Air Act improvement efforts that I thought I would share. Funny, but some of these sayings I heard Mom say tens and tens of times.

- ❖ "All shall be well and all shall be well, and all manner of things shall be well."--Julian of Norwich
- ❖ "I'm not called to be successful, I'm called to be faithful."--Mother Teresa
- ❖ "The Lord is near to the broken-hearted, and saves the crushed in spirit."--Psalm 34
- ❖ "There are no ordinary people."--C.S. Lewis
- ❖ "I just came to paint."--Bob German (family friend)
- ❖ "He has showed you, o man, what is good; and what doth the Lord require you but to do justice, love mercy, and walk humbly with thy God."--Micah 5
- ❖ "Work like you don't need the money. Love like you've never been hurt. Dance like nobody's watching."--Unknown
- ❖ "Imagination is more important than knowledge."--Einstein
- ❖ "Walk on a rainbow trail; walk on a trail of song, and all about you will be beauty. There is a way out of every dark mist, over a rainbow trail."--Navajo Song
- ❖ "Real isn't how you are made," said the Skin Horse. "It's a thing that happens to you. When a child loves you for a long, long time, not just to play with, but REALLY loves you, then you become Real."
"Does it hurt?" asked the Rabbit.
"Sometimes," said the Skin Horse, for he was always truthful. "When you are Real you don't mind being hurt."
"Does it happen all at once, like being wound up," he asked, "or bit by bit?"
"It doesn't happen all at once," said the Skin Horse. "You become. It takes a long time. That's why it doesn't happen often to people who break easily, or have sharp edges, or who have to be carefully kept. Generally, by the time you are Real, most of your hair has been loved off, and your eyes drop out and you get loose in the joints and

very shabby. But these things don't matter at all, because once you are Real you can't be ugly, except to people who don't understand.[. . .] Once you are REAL, you can't become unreal again. It lasts forever."--The Velveteen Rabbit, Marjory Williams

❖ "Doubt is merely the seed of faith, a sign that faith is alive and ready to grow."--Kathleen Norris

❖ "The journey of a thousand miles begins with the first step."--Lao Tse

❖ Lord, make me a channel of thy peace;
that where there is hatred, I may bring love;
that where there is wrong, I may bring the spirit of forgiveness;
that where there is discord, I may bring harmony;
that where there is error, I may bring truth;
that where there is doubt, I may bring faith;
that where there is despair, I may bring hope;
that where there are shadows, I may bring light;
that where there is sadness, I may bring joy.
Lord, grant that I may seek rather to comfort than to be comforted;
to understand, than to be understood;
to love, than to be loved.
For it is by self-forgetting that one finds.
It is by forgiving that one is forgiven.
It is by dying that one awakens to eternal life.
Amen.--**St. Francis**

❖ "Dam the torpedos; full speed ahead."--Admiral Farragut

I Can

Congress and powerful people might not be able to simplify and revitalize the Clean Air Act . . . but I can.

-----"Impossible is just a big word thrown around by small men who find it easier to live in the world they've been given than to explore the power they have to change it. Impossible is not a fact. It's an opinion. Impossible is not a declaration. It's a dare. Impossible is potential. Impossible is temporary. Impossible is nothing."— Muhammad Ali

Reasons Why the Clean Air Act cannot be Reformed

Sentiment: "We need to fix Congress before we can fix the Clean Air Act."

Sentiment: "We need a more cooperative Congress before we can fix the Clean Air Act."

Hogwash.

Liking thinking that if we just had $1 million, or lived somewhere else, or had a spouse that was more loving to us--we could really take that next step in life. Hogwash. Self-imprisonment. This thinking will get you nowhere. Trust me. I've tried it. Fight this thinking like a disease.

> ---"Ninety-nine percent of the failures come from people who have the habit of making excuses." ---George Washington Carver

> ---"Love will find a way. Indifference will find an excuse."---Anonymous

Biggest Obstacle to Clean Air Act Reform

Probably the biggest initial impediment to overcoming our problems, whether they be with the Clean Air Act or with some other element of our life, is not a lack of self-discipline, but a lack of self-laughter. Congress wants to bemoan its brokenness. I want to bemoan my brokenness. Let's all just have a laugh. We are silly people. All will be well.

Too Many Problems . . . I can't Handle It Any More

Sentiment: . . . problems with the Clean Air Act . . . problems with my life; . . . It's just too much.

> Lo! now thy swift dogs, over stone and bush,
> After me, straying sheep, loud barking, rush.
> There's Fear, and Shame, and Empty-heart, and Lack,
> And Lost-love, and a thousand at their back!
> I see thee not, but know thou hound'st them on,

And I am lost indeed--escape is none.
See! there they come, down streaming on my track!

I rise and run, staggering--double and run.--
But whither?--whither?--whither for escape?
The sea lies all about this long-necked cape--
There come the dogs, straight for me every one--
Me, live despair, live centre of alarms!--
Ah! lo! 'twixt me and all his barking harms,
The shepherd, lo!--I run--fall folded in his arms.

There let the dogs yelp, let them growl and leap;
It is no matter--I will go to sleep.
Like a spent cloud pass pain and grief and fear,
Out from behind it unchanged love shines clear.

[. . .]

Destroy my darkness, rise my perfect joy;
Love primal, the live coal of every night,
Flame out, scare the ill things with radiant fright,
And fill my tent with laughing morn's delight.

[. . .]

How we grow weary plodding on the way;
Of future joy how present pain bereaves,
Rounding us with a dark of mere decay,
Tossed with a drift of summer-fallen leaves.

Thou knowest all our weeping, fainting, striving;
Thou know'st how very hard it is to be;
How hard to rouse faint will not yet reviving;
To do the pure thing, trusting all to thee;
To hold thou art there, for all no face we see;
How hard to think, through cold and dark and dearth,
That thou art nearer now than when eye-seen on earth.

Have pity on us for the look of things,
When blank denial stares us in the face.
Although the serpent mask have lied before,

It fascinates the bird that darkling sings,
And numbs the little prayer-bird's beating wings.
For how believe thee somewhere in blank space,
If through the darkness come no knocking to our door?

If we might sit until the darkness go,
Possess our souls in patience perhaps we might;
But there is always something to be done,
And no heart left to do it. To and fro
The dull thought surges, as the driven waves fight
In gulfy channels. Oh! victorious one,
Give strength to rise, go out, and meet thee in the night.

"Wake, thou that sleepest; rise up from the dead,
And Christ will give thee light." I do not know
What sleep is, what is death, or what is light;
But I am waked enough to feel a woe,
To rise and leave death. Stumbling through the night,
To my dim lattice, O calling Christ! I go,
And out into the dark look for thy star-crowned head.

[. . .]

I let all run:--set thou and trim my sails;
Home then my course, let blow whatever gales.

With thee on board, each sailor is a king
Nor I mere captain of my vessel then,
But heir of earth and heaven, eternal child;
Daring all truth, nor fearing anything;
Mighty in love, the servant of all men;
Resenting nothing, taking rage and blare
Into the Godlike silence of a loving care.

       ---George MacDonald, "A Book of Strife in the Form of The Diary of an Old Soul"

Progress

Sentiment: "I can't see it. I can't see any progress."

Probably a good thing. If this thing down here's supposed to work mostly by faith and not by sight, probably a good thing if we aren't seeing much.

My 8-year old the other night said, "Dad, just because you can't see it doesn't mean that it doesn't exist."

Probably right son.

> ----"Help me to walk by the other light supreme, which shows thy facts behind man's vaguely hinting dream."---George MacDonald

Fixing the Clean Air Act

Sentiment: "Congress can't fix the Clean Air Act right now. It's impossible."

I hear this all the time. I even hear it from members of Congress. The world even commends people for thinking this way. "That lady really knows what's going on." "That guy is a practical thinker." "That person is sure grounded in reality." Seems strange to me. Like commending someone for diagnosing a flat tire. Quite obvious. Not commendable to diagnose a flat tire. Commendable to try to fix a flat tire even if the odds are completely against you.

I bet all of you have tried to help someone along the road of life even though you knew you were likely to fail. And even when you failed, did you really fail? I bet you gained from your effort--and I bet the other person appreciated the fact that you tried even though they also knew you were likely to fail.

People can sit around and talk about the impossibilities of fixing the flat tire. I'll take a 4-year old with a tire iron.

Weariness from the Battle

Ever get so weary of the battles, be they over the Clean Air Act or some other aspect of life, that you want to just give-up on it all?

Me too.

Difficult.

Painful.

Here's the crazy thing though. Seems like it might be in these moments that the world can be most easily overcome--and true joy potentially realized. Perhaps it's just an ugly, wonderful, loving gift.

----'Lo I am weary unto death! The battle is gone from me! It is lost, or unworth gaining! The world is too much for me! Its forces will not heed me! They have worn me out! I have wrought no salvation even for my own, and never should work any, were I to live forever! It is enough; let me now return whence I came; let me be gathered to my fathers and be at rest!'?

I should be loth to think that, if the enemy, in recognizable shape, came roaring upon us, we would not, like the red-cross knight, stagger, heavy sword in nerveless arm, to meet him; but, in the feebleness of foiled effort, it wants yet more faith to rise and partake of the food that shall bring back more effort, more travail, more weariness. The true man trusts in a strength which is not his, and which he does not feel, does not even always desire; believes in a power that seems far from him, which is yet at the root of his fatigue itself and his need of rest—rest as far from death as is labour. To trust in the strength of God in our weakness; to say, 'I am weak: so let me be: God is strong;' to seek from him who is our life, as the natural, simple cure of all that is amiss with us, power to do, and be, and live, even

when we are weary,—this is the victory that overcometh the world. To believe in God our strength in the face of all seeming denial, to believe in him out of the heart of weakness and unbelief, in spite of numbness and weariness and lethargy; to believe in the wide-awake real, through all the stupefying, enervating, distorting dream; to will to wake, when the very being seems athirst for a godless repose;—these are the broken steps up to the high fields where repose is but a form of strength, strength but a form of joy, joy but a form of love. 'I am weak,' says the true soul, 'but not so weak that I would not be strong; not so sleepy that I would not see the sun rise; not so lame but that I would walk! Thanks be to him who perfects strength in weakness, and gives to his beloved while they sleep!'--- George MacDonald

Plagiarism

One of you asked to borrow some of my slides. You bet! Replicate them, revise them, add to them--do whatever you want with them. Most of all I hope you add your own light to them. I don't consider them to be mine. 99% of my best work is plagiarized.

- "Good artists copy, great artists steal."--Picasso

- "Originality is undetected plagiarism."--William Ralph Inge

- "It takes a thousand men to invent a telegraph, or a steam engine, or a phonograph, or a photograph, or a telephone or any other important thing—and the last man gets the credit and we forget the others. He added his little mite — that is all he did. These object lessons should teach us that ninety-nine parts of all things that proceed from the intellect are

plagiarisms, pure and simple; and the lesson ought to make us modest. But nothing can do that." —Mark Twain

- "All my best thoughts were stolen from the ancients."--Emerson

- "We are like dwarfs sitting on the shoulders of giants. We see more, and things that are more distant, than they did, not because our sight is superior or because we are taller than they, but because they raise us up, and by their great stature add to ours."--John of Salisbury

- "It's often a shock to the thinking person when they find that their revolutionary new idea is not new at all. Most likely, someone in a robe thought of it thousands of years ago."--Anonymous

- "It is the little writer rather than the great writer who seems never to quote, and the reason is that he is never really doing anything else."--Havelock Ellis

- "Immature poets imitate; mature poets steal."--T.S. Eliot

Biggest Obstacle to Clean Air Act Reform

Biggest obstacle to Clean Air Act reform that I'm finding isn't Congress, but Self. Surmountable though. And intriguing that this approach would seem to result in more meaningful and far-reaching consequences than Clean Air Act reform. Might need to give it more of a try.

- "This love of our neighbour is the only door out of the dungeon of self, where we mope and mow, striking sparks, and rubbing phosphorescences out of the walls, and blowing our own breath in our own nostrils, instead of issuing to the fair sunlight of God, the sweet winds of the universe. The man thinks his consciousness is himself; whereas his life consisteth in the inbreathing of God, and the consciousness of the universe of truth. To have himself, to know himself, to enjoy himself, he calls life; whereas, if he would forget himself, tenfold would be his life in God

and his neighbours. The region of man's life is a spiritual region. God, his friends, his neighbours, his brothers all, is the wide world in which alone his spirit can find room. Himself is his dungeon. If he feels it not now, he will yet feel it one day—feel it as a living soul would feel being prisoned in a dead body, wrapped in sevenfold cerements, and buried in a stone-ribbed vault within the last ripple of the sound of the chanting people in the church above. His life is not in knowing that he lives, but in loving all forms of life. He is made for the All, for God, who is the All, is his life. And the essential joy of his life lies abroad in the liberty of the All. His delights, like those of the Ideal Wisdom, are with the sons of men. His health is in the body of which the Son of Man is the head. The whole region of life is open to him—nay, he must live in it or perish.

- "Nor thus shall a man lose the consciousness of well-being. Far deeper and more complete, God and his neighbour will flash it back upon him— pure as life. No more will he agonize "with sick assay" to generate it in the light of his own decadence. For he shall know the glory of his own being in the light of God and of his brother."---George MacDonald

- "All the doors that lead inward to the secret place of the Most High are doors outward, out of self, out of smallness, out of wrong."---George MacDonald

Percentage of Environmental Degradation Due to the Complexity of the Regulatory System

Read these statistics. Then tell me the percentage of companies you think are currently in violation an air quality requirement because, in part, the company does not understand how a rule works . . . or even that a particular requirement exists?

> "Half of the gadgets returned to stores (and the cost of returned products in America, they estimate, is some $100 billion a year) are "in good working order, but customers can't figure out how to operate them."

> ➤ "80 percent of child safety seats are improperly installed or misused and the instructions for installing them are the root of the problem."

> ----- "My suggestion is that governments can serve their citizens a lot better if they get simpler."--Cass Sunstein

Time to simplify the Clean Air Act. We can make it happen.

It is Well

Anyone who thinks that strength is not manifest in weakness has not read the story of Horatio Spafford. When Clean Air Act controversies or life gets you down . . . just think of the story of Horatio Spafford and the words he chose to pen as his ship passed where the SS Ville du Havre sank. Unimaginable.

Horatio Spafford

In 1870, Horatio's only son died of Scarlet Fever. In 1871, the Great Chicago Fire ruined him financially (he had been a successful lawyer and had invested significantly in property decimated by the great fire). In 1873, his business interests were further hit by the economic downturn at which time he had planned to travel to Europe with his family on the SS Ville du Havre. In a late change of plan, he sent the family ahead while he was delayed on business concerning zoning problems following the Great Chicago Fire. While crossing the Atlantic, the ship sank and all four of Spafford's daughters died. His wife Anna survived and sent him the now famous telegram, "**Saved alone ...**".
Shortly afterwards, as Spafford traveled to Europe to meet his grieving wife, he was inspired to write these words as his ship passed near where his daughters had died:

It Is Well With My Soul

When peace like a river attendeth my way,
 When sorrows like sea billows roll;
Whatever my lot Thou hast taught me to say,
 "It is well, it is well with my soul!"

It is well with my soul!
It is well, it is well with my soul!

Though Satan should buffet, though trials should come,

Let this blest assurance control,
That Christ hath regarded my helpless estate,
 And hath shed His own blood for my soul.

My sin—oh, the bliss of this glorious thought—
 My sin, not in part, but the whole,
Is nailed to His Cross, and I bear it no more;
 Praise the Lord, praise the Lord, O my soul!
And, Lord, haste the day when my faith shall be sight,
the clouds be rolled back as a scroll;
the trump shall resound, and the Lord shall descend,
even so, it is well with my soul

Navy SEAL Traning and the Clean Air Act

Whether we are battling cancer, Clean Air Act transformation, family problems, or other challenges—there are some interesting Navy SEAL tips to help resist the tendency to want to give up and to relieve stress.

The technique that resonated most with me was to *"embrace the suck"*. I remember that a sports writer watching the tribal Tarahumura run once said that one of the most defining characteristics of these superhuman ultra-marathoners is that around Mile Marker 50 . . . they start to smile.

Failure to Transform the Clean Air Act

"You people have spent over 10 years trying to transform the Clean Air Act— all of which has failed."

That's correct.

> -------"To help the growth of a thought that struggles toward the light; to brush with gentle hand the stain from the white of one snowdrop— such be my ambition."— George Macdonald.

Life, Difficulty, and the Clean Air Act

Life is difficult. It's got its joys—but it's difficult. If you haven't figure this out, either you haven't lived long enough or are deadening your senses to experience. Here's the deal though. Once we acknowledge it's difficult, it starts to lose its difficulty.

> ---"Life is difficult. This is a great truth, one of the greatest truths. It is a great truth because when we truly see this truth we transcend it. Once we truly know that life is difficult, once we truly understand and accept it, then life is no longer difficult. Because once it is accepted, the fact that life is difficult no longer matters."---M. Scott Peck

Where should we aim?

The easiest and best way to improve the Clean Air Act is not to ultimately aim at improving the Clean Air Act.

> ----"Aim at heaven and you will get earth thrown in. Aim at earth and you get neither."—C.S. Lewis

Love, Truth, and the Clean Air Act

How can I bring up spiritual terms, such as love and truth, into a discussion of the Clean Air Act?

I'm not sure if there is anything, at its root, that is not an affair of the spirit.

Bearing More Fruit

How do you create a Clean Air Act that bears more fruit and new kinds of fruit?

Often the answer to life's questions are written very simply in nature. How do you get a tree to bear more abundant and new kinds of fruit?

Prune and graft.

Must be both dying and adding new life. Can't just prune. That doesn't allow new fruits to grow. Can't just graft. That doesn't remove the branches that no longer bear fruit and draw nourishment away from the tree.

If you want the Clean Air Act to produce more fruit, and new kinds of fruit such as addressing climate change, remove 50-75% of the dead branches and graft in a new branch such as a multi-pollutant market-based system based on real-time source monitoring that would allow businesses to react quicker to market opportunities.

> — "Is it really necessary to prune the grape vines?
> If you would like to collect more than one cluster of grapes, yes! Here is why: the vine will only be producing fruit on the new branches of the year. If you let the vine make five meters of branches every year, after 3 years your vine will have to feed 15 meters of branches to reach the branch's extremity where the fruit are! The vine will not have much energy left when it comes to the end of the branch, hence the fruit yield will be very low. Pruning your vine is essential, because it limits the amount of useless branches to feed (read: branches not producing fruit)."---*Hardy Fruit Trees*

Let's prune, graft, and watch this tree flourish.

Most Radical Words to Speak in these Clean Air Act Controversies

The most radical words to speak in all these Clean Air Act controversies is to say "all is well".

Almost everything around is saying that things are not well. To say "all is well" is therefore completely radical. In fact it appears insane on the surface. How can we say "all is well" when things clearly are not well?

I think we only perceive a small amount of what is actually happening. There seems to me to be an undercurrent of love and truth that exists below the surface that makes up the bulk of existence, but to which we only catch occasional glimpses of.

-----"When I see the blind and wretched state of men, when I survey the whole universe in its deadness, and man left to himself with no light, as though lost in this corner of the universe without knowing who put him there, what he has to do, or what will become of him when he dies, incapable of knowing anything, I am moved to terror, like a man transported in his sleep to some terrifying desert island, who wakes up quite lost, with no means of escape. Then I marvel that so wretched a state does not drive people to despair. I see other people around me, made like myself. I ask them if that are any better informed than I, and they say they are not. Then these lost and wretched creatures look around and find some attractive objects to which they have become addicted and attached. For my part, I have never been able to form attachments, and considering how very likely it is that there exists something besides what I can see, I have tried to find out whether God has left any traces of himself."

----Blaise Pascal

Two possibilities it seems. Either there is this current of good below the surface—guiding us toward its end. Or there isn't. I choose to believe the former.

Getting into Trouble and the Clean Air Act

Some people don't want to get involved in improving the Clean Air Act because they do not want to get into trouble. Seems like we're supposed to get in trouble.

"Jesus promised his disciples three things—that they would be completely fearless, absurdly happy, and in constant trouble."—G.K. Chesterton

Love and the Clean Air Act

"Doesn't it bother you to be hated by so many people both on the left and the right of this issue".

Of course. But in truth it's of little consequence. In the end I don't think the question will be how much we were loved—but how much we loved. The answer to this question is what will truly bother me. I've got a long way to go.

> With thee on board, each sailor is king
> Nor I mere captain of my vessel then,
> But hear of earth and heaven, eternal child;
> Daring all truth, nor fearing anything;
> Mighty in love, the servant of all men;
> Resenting nothing, taking rage and blare
> Into the Godlike silence of a loving care.
> ---George MacDonald

Which is More Complicated? The Atmosphere or Clean Air Act?

What is more difficult to understand? The atmosphere or the Clean Air Act?

Atmospheric chemistry and meteorology are extremely complicated—but they must follow the rules of nature and logic. Though we do not yet fully understand them yet—they are understandable. The Clean Air Act however is not so bound. And being a neuroscientist as Gina McCarthy suggested, or even an astrophysicist, will not allow us to comprehend how in reality the Clean Air Act works. I'll prove this to you. Einstein might have been able to figure out the space-time continuum, but Einstein could never have figured out what constitutes a "site" for Title V purposes.

The Clean Air Act should work simpler than the atmosphere. Let's make it happen.

Science Loves Simplicity

❖ "I'll tell you what you need to be a great scientist. You don't have to be able understand very complicated things. It's just the opposite. You have to be able to see what looks like the most complicated thing in the world and, in a flash, find the underlying simplicity. That's what you need: a talent for simplicity."— *Mitchell Wilson*

- ❖ "Science may be described as the art of systematic over-simplification."— *Karl Popper*
- ❖ "You know you've achieved perfection in design, not when you have nothing more to add, but when you have nothing more to take away.'— *Antoine de Saint-Exupéry*
- ❖ "Fools ignore complexity; pragmatists suffer it; experts avoid it; geniuses remove it."- *Alan Perlis*
- ❖ "Simplifications have had a much greater long-range scientific impact than individual feats of ingenuity. The opportunity for simplification is very encouraging, because in all examples that come to mind the simple and elegant systems tend to be easier and faster to design and get right, more efficient in execution, and much more reliable than the more contrived contraptions that have to be debugged into some degree of acceptability.... Simplicity and elegance are unpopular because they require hard work and discipline to achieve and education to be appreciated."-- *Edsger W. Dijkstra*
- ❖ "If you can't reduce a difficult engineering problem to just one 8-1/2 x 11-inch sheet of paper, you will probably never understand it." Ralph Brazelton Peck
- ❖ "[T]he grand aim of all science...is to cover the greatest possible number of empirical facts by logical deductions from the smallest possible number of hypotheses or axioms."---Albert Einstein
- ❖ "Complexity is a sign of technical immaturity. Simplicity of use is the real sign of a well design product whether it is an ATM or a Patriot missile."-- *Daniel T. Ling*
- ❖ "Remember that there is no code faster than no code."-- *Taligent's Guide to Designing Programs*
- ❖ "Simplicity is prerequisite for reliability."-- *Edsger W.Dijkstra*
- ❖ "Phenomena complex—laws simple."— *Richard P. Feynman*
- ❖ "The cheapest, fastest, and most reliable components of a computer system are those that aren't there."-- *Graham Bell*
- ❖ "When Henry Ford decided to produce his famous V-8 motor, he chose to build an engine with the entire eight cylinders cast in one block, and instructed his engineers to produce a design for the engine. The design was placed on paper, but the engineers agreed, to a man, that it was simply impossible to cast an eight-cylinder engine-block in one piece. Ford replied,"Produce it anyway." — Henry Ford
- ❖ "Simplicity does not precede complexity, but follows it."- *Alan J. Perlis*

- ❖ "The main purpose of science is simplicity and as we understand more things, everything is becoming simpler." - Edward Teller
- ❖ "Simplicity is the ultimate sophistication." Leonardo da Vinci
- ❖ "There's an old story about the person who wished his computer were as easy to use as his telephone. That wish has come true, since I no longer know how to use my telephone."-- *Bjarne Stroustrup*
- ❖ "There are two ways of constructing a software design. One way is to make it so simple that there are obviously no deficiencies. And the other way is to make it so complicated that there are no obvious deficiencies."-- *C.A.R. Hoare*
- ❖ "Nature operates in the shortest way possible."--Aristotle
- ❖ "Nature does not multiply things unnecessarily; that she makes use of the easiest and simplest means for producing her effects; that she does nothing in vain, and the like".—Galileo
- ❖ "Five lines where three are enough is stupidity. Nine pounds where three are sufficient is stupidity."—Frank Lloyd Wright
- ❖ "Rudiments or principles must not be unnecessarily multiplied (entia praeter necessitatem non esse multiplicanda)—Immanuel Kant
- ❖ "Don't be fooled by the many books on complexity or by the many complex and arcane algorithms you find in this book or elsewhere. Although there are no textbooks on simplicity, simple systems work and complex don't." ---Jim Gray
- ❖ "Truth is ever to be found in simplicity, and not in the multiplicity and confusion of things."---Isaac Newton

Guy in a T-Shirt and Shorts Re-Writes Clean Air Act

"It's impossible to re-write the Clean Air Act."

Can't be. I did it. And I re-wrote it in a t-shirt and shorts sitting around my house.

If someone as small, weak, and insignificant as I am can re-write the Clean Air Act . . . can't be impossible.

Not impossible.

----"It always seems impossible until its done."--- Nelson Mandela

----"We would accomplish many more things if we did not think of them as impossible."---Vince Lombardi
----"It's kind of fun to do the impossible."---Walt Disney

A Perfect Clean Air Act

I'd like to see no more pollution, no more environmental laws, and a situation where companies can make billions of dollars making wonderful products for me to use and enjoy.

> "Gentleman, we will chase perfection, and we will chase it relentlessly knowing all the while we can excellence." - Vince Lombardi

Easier than it Looks—Simplifying the Clean Air Act

I bet many people think about simplifying the Clean Air Act but look at the accomplishments of Einstein, Steve Jobs, Isaac Newton, and Thoreau that were manifested through their focus on simplicity and say, "Yeah, but they were geniuses". These people would likely tell you they were largely plagiarists. See any difference between the following quotes:

> — "Simplicity is the ultimate sophistication." — Leonardo da Vinci

> — "Simplicity is the ultimate sophistication."—Steve Jobs

Emerson once wrote, "All my best thoughts were stolen from the ancients." Picasso once said, "Good artists copy, great artists steal". People call it genius, but as you can see it's largely not—and all of us are capable of it.

Want to know how to simplify the Clean Air Act? Just steel a few hundred pounds of thought from the ancients, add one ounce of your own, and change the wrapping paper.

---"Thousands of geniuses live and die undiscovered--either by themselves or by others."--- Mark Twain

Comfort and Security

It's interesting that we seek comfort and security in our professional lives—yet these are not qualities we admire in a person.

> ❖ "I have never in my life envied a human being who led an easy life. I have envied a great many people who led difficult lives and led them well."— Theodore Roosevelt

Professional Guilt and the Clean Air Act

Anyone feel guilty for taking people's money to do a bunch of this stuff?

I've made hundreds of thousands of dollars for example just performing common control analyses and netting exercises. I'm happy to help clients with these issues—but part of me feels guilty for taking people's money to perform these unnecessarily complicated analyses and then turning around and trying to convince my conscience—"Well . . . that's just the way the system works".

Hair cutting seems to be an honest profession. You give someone a haircut and 100% of what you earned was necessary to perform.

I'm not sure if I'm at 25%.

Three responses. One is to keep taking people's money and keep your mouth shut. Second is to remain in the system but open your mouth and suggest that the system be simplified as we all know it now can be. Third is to become a hair stylist.

The Truth that Breaks the Chains

To go beyond human strength and endurance in any endeavor, including reforming the Clean Air Act, requires the acceptance of one truth that puts everything within reach—you are loved.

The Price of Improving the Clean Air Act

"If I try to help my country by improving the Clean Air Act even though almost everyone says it can't be done---people will laugh at me, ignore me, and despise me."

That's correct. Cheap price compared to what others have been willing to pay for their country. Much easier to be laughed at than shot at.

Too Busy to Reform the Clean Air Act

"I'm too busy implementing the Clean Air Act to talk about changing it."

> A man saw another man digging a hole with his hands and said, "Hey, why don't you look for a shovel?". The man replied, "I can't right now. I'm too busy digging this hole."

The Waiting Place

Everyone realize that Congress is waiting for us to fix the Clean Air Act?

Congress is waiting for us.

We are waiting for them.

Everyone is just waiting.

"But somehow we'll escape all the waiting and staying and find the bright places where Boom Bands are playing!'—Dr. Seuss

> ----"*Action springs not from thought, but from a readiness for responsibility.*"---Dietrich Boenhoeffer

Failing

"We have failed to transform the Clean Air Act." Nope. Can never fail at anything in life unless you quit.

> --------"*You never fail until you stop trying.*"----Albert Einstein

Maybe We are Wrong

Maybe we are wrong for trying to transform the Clean Air Act. Maybe history will reveal that our purpose did not resonate with the truth—and our nation's reliance on the Clean Air Act was the best approach to cleaning the air.

That will be just fine.

> "Let a man do right, nor trouble himself about worthless opinion; the less he heeds tongues, the less difficult will he find it to love men. Let him comfort himself with the thought that the truth must out. He will not have to pass through eternity with the brand of ignorant or malicious judgment upon him. He shall find his peers and be judged of them. "But, thou who lookest for the justification of the light, art thou verily prepared for thyself to encounter such exposure as the general unveiling of things must bring? Art thou willing for the truth whatever it be? I nowise mean to ask, Have you a conscience so void of offence, have you a heart so pure and clean, that you fear no fullest exposure of what is in you to the gaze of men and angels?—as to God, he knows it all now! What I mean to ask is, Do you so love the truth and the right, that you welcome, or at least submit willingly to the idea of an exposure of what in you is yet unknown to yourself-an exposure that may redound to the glory of the truth by making you ashamed and humble? It may be, for instance, that you were wrong in regard to those, for the righting of whose wrongs to you, the great judgment of God is now by you waited for with desire: will you welcome any discovery, even if it work for the excuse of others, that will make you more true, by revealing what in you was false? Are you willing to be made glad that you were wrong when you thought others were wrong? If you can with such submission face the revelation of things hid, then you are of the truth, and need not be afraid; for, whatever comes, it will and can only make you more true and humble and pure."—George MacDonald

The Better Investment

I've made hundreds of thousands of dollars due in large part to the needless complexity and brokenness of the current Clean Air Act. Is this ok? I don't

know. I do know this though. I will be gone. Might be 60 years from now. Might be tomorrow. But I will be gone. What will remain is the truth. To the extent I have contributed to the truth what I do will live on—not as myself—but as the truth. To the extent I haven't—I have little doubt my actions are destined for the ash heap of time.

----*"Death cancels everything but truth."*—Proverb

Evolution and the Clean Air Act

----"One always begins with the simple, then comes the complex, and by superior enlightenment one often reverts in the end to the simple. Such is the course of human intelligence." ---Voltaire

Such will be with the Clean Air Act.

Want to Change the Clean Air Act?

Quite easy. Just pick up your pen.

-----"If you want to change the world, pick up your pen and write." ----Martin Luther

One Question

Ask yourself one question about the Clean Air Act. Are the solutions in the Clean Air Act as simple as they can be?

------"When the solution is simple, God is answering."---Albert Einstein

Not Enough Time

"We might not be around long enough for these Clean Air Act reforms to get through."

True.

But we also might not be around long enough to go to the grocery store tomorrow.

Accomplishments in the end I think will be relatively meaningless. What will matter most is that we tried.

Difficult, Lonely, and Treacherous

Listen. I understand that reforming the Clean Air Act is difficult. I understand it is lonely. I understand that people will make fun of you. I understand you will get beat-up. Isn't it wonderful!!! What a great gift it is to be treated this way—whether its deserved or undeserved.

At the end of all this I hope we can all sit around drinking a beer together, all tired, all torn up, and say as Mother Pollard said during the Montgomery Bus Boycott---"My feets is tired. But my soul is rested."

Words Speak Louder than Action

Many people want to help reform the Clean Air Act, but they don't know where to begin. It's quite easy. Just talk and write about it. Words are our action. Actions do not speak louder than words in our profession-- otherwise what would count most is how well we typed and read a computer screen. Words are our action. The best way for us to therefore walk the talk is to talk the walk.

The First Step

From what I'm hearing, the main reason for not changing the Clean Air Act is fear:

> ➤ Environmental groups fear if the Clean Air Act is changed it will be weakened.
> ➤ Business groups fear if the Clean Air Act is changed it will be strengthened.
> ➤ Regulators and environmental professionals fear if the Clean Air Act is changed our livelihoods will be endangered.

It's comforting to hear that the main reason for not changing the Clean Air Act is fear. Why? Because fear is easily surmounted. There is a simple antidote. Courage. And courage is easy to obtain. It just comes naturally with the first step.

I think many people mistakenly believe that courage precedes action, but courage does not precede action, it's just action necessitating courage. Most people that have done something courageous (which I believe is all of us) will tell you that they did not feel courageous before taking the action, they just took the first small step and the courage followed.
The courage will follow. Let's take the first step. Time to transform the Clean Air Act. We can make it happen.

Call to Protect the Clean Air Act

People are calling for the Clean Air Act to be protected. I understand the intent, but I wanted to point out that sometimes by protecting something we can do more harm to that which we are trying to protect. As Robert Frost once wrote in the poem *the Mending Wall*—"Before I built a wall I'd ask to know what I was walling in or walling out, And to whom I was likely to give offence."

Life requires death. New growth requires the removal of branches that no longer bear abundant fruit. Walls unfortunately do not discriminate. They may keep out the rabbits, but they also keep out the gardener and limit the garden. Instead of protecting the Clean Air Act, let's jump in there together and prune it, add some water, and watch it bear even more plentiful and healthier fruit.

It's a "Small Multi-Pollutant World After All"

Though we should think globally and act locally, we should not make the locally responsible for justifying to the nationally the part of globally that the locally cannot do. Harder to act locally if you are busy globalling.

Martin Luther King Day

I don't know about you, but too often I've chosen comfort and respectability over trying to do what was right—with regard to the Clean Air Act and other things. On this day I am reminded again of the other path.

From Martin Luther King's speech the "Transformed Nonconformist":

> Success, recognition, and conformity are the bywords of the modern world where everyone seems to crave the anaesthetizing security of being identified with the majority. In spite of this prevailing tendency to conform, we as Christians have a mandate to be nonconformists. The Apostle Paul, who knew the inner realities of the Christian faith, counseled, "Be not conformed to this world: but be ye transformed by the renewing of your mind." We are called to be people of conviction, not conformity; of moral nobility, not social respectability. We are commanded to live differently and according to a higher loyalty. [. . .]
>
> The hope of a secure and livable world lies with disciplined nonconformists, who are dedicated to justice, peace, and brotherhood. The trailblazers in human, academic, scientific, and religious freedom have always been nonconformists. In any cause that concerns the progress of mankind, put your faith in the nonconformist! In his essay "Self-Reliance" Emerson wrote, "Whoso would be a man must be a nonconformist. The Apostle Paul reminds us that whoso would be a Christian must also be a nonconformist. Any Christian who blindly accepts the opinions of the majority and in fear and timidity follows a path of expediency and social approval is a mental and spiritual slave. Mark well these words from the pen of James Russel Lowell:
>
>> They are slaves who fear to speak
>> For the fallen and the weak;
>> They are slaves who wil not choose
>> Hatred, scoffing, and abuse,
>> Rather than in silence shrink
>> From the truth they needs must think;
>> They are slaves who dare not be
>> In the right with two or three. [. . .]
>
> We must make a choice. Will we continue to march to the drumbeat of conformity and respectability, or will we, listening to the beat of a more distant drum, move to its echoing sounds? Will we march only to the music of time, or will we, risking criticism and abuse, march to

the soul-saving music of eternity? More than ever before we are today challenged by the words of yesterday, "Be not conformed to this world: but be ye transformed by the renewing of your mind.

The New Congress and Clean Air Act Reform

A couple people asked me whether I thought the new Congress will be more apt to transform the Clean Air Act. I don't know. I do know this though. The only way to transform the Clean Air Act is to focus on me—not them. I cannot control what they do. I can however control what I do. The more relevant question therefore is whether I will be more apt to transform the Clean Air Act.

Success might be outside our control. Effort however is not.

> ----- "God doesn't require us to succeed, he only requires that you try". – Mother Teresa

And what's wonderful is that it is in this trying where we will find the reward.

> -----*"Satisfaction does not come with achievement, but with effort. Full effort is full victory."* --Mahatma Gandhi

On to effort. On to victory.

Pace of Clean Air Act Reform

I think I'm starting to understand why the Clean Air Act is not being reformed very quickly. Seems like it is so complicated and removed from the public that most people don't understand what's happening—and the people who do understand what's happening all derive money and power from its brokenness. Think about it. It's kind of crazy. But the more complicated, bigger, and messy the Clean Air Act gets—the more money and power each of us stands to gain. This is true for all of us—including the attorneys, the consultants, the environmental groups, the environmental company representatives, and the agency personnel. The fact is that if the Clean Air Act is transformed into a more effective, efficient process all of us stand to lose power and money. So why would we want to transform the

Clean Air Act? I can only speak for myself. Just seems like the right thing to do. That and I've never seen a hearse pulling a U-haul.

> -----"It is difficult to get a man to understand something when his salary depends upon his not understanding it." -- Upton Sinclair: (1878-1968) US novelist

Time to transform the Clean Air Act. We all will still have plenty to do. Let's make it happen.

Size of the Clean Air Act

We seem to be focused only on things that will make the Clean Air Act bigger and more complex. Imagine if the people who built the Apple Ipod concentrated only on its capabilities and not also on its size, simplicity, and ease of use?

Hard to go running with a Juke Box on your back.

Art Buchwald

When we think of how the Clean Air Act will be changed I think we envision some powerful and influential person, who understands the Clean Air Act much better than we do, giving a rousing speech before Congress that convinces Congress than an update is needed. That's not however how the Clean Air Act will likely be changed. Here is a much more likely scenario:

> Chris's 5-year old will wet the bed at 3:30 a.m. one night. Chris won't be able to go back to sleep and will jot a note on his nightstand about an idea for updating the Clean Air Act. When Chris gets to work he will write an email to Jed. Jed will think, "that's a great idea, I'll put it in a presentation." John will be at the presentation and will be encouraged that others are thinking about the Clean Air Act. Afterwards John will call Jennifer, "Hey Jennifer, I remember you wrote a paper on the Clean Air Act a few years ago—I just heard someone with a similar idea". Jennifer will then be encouraged to start writing again. Jennifer's newest blog entry will be read by a Congressional staffer who at that moment in time is preparing questions for a Congressional panel. One of the Congressional

panelists, Carlos, will then answer the question that a few months later convinces a Congresswoman that she should sponsor an amendment to update the Clean Air Act.

That's how the Clean Air Act will be changed.

Question: In the above proximate chain of events, would the Clean Air Act have been changed but for Chris, Jed, John, Jennifer, or Susana? The answer is no. It would not. I'm sorry this will not come with fanfare and praises for jotting a note at 3:30 am, sending an email, or encouraging someone to write about the Clean Air Act again. It's just not how it works. Two comments on this though. First, you can't take worldly praise with you anyway—and none of us are going to be here for very long—it's just a fact. And second, praise can be one the biggest impediments to what I think we truly want (e.g. the peace and joy that comes in part with the removal of pride and self). Moreover, the greatest thing is this. All of the fun and reward is in the doing, not in the achieving. Anyone run or walk a 5k? Is the fun in crossing the finish-line, or in the doing? The fun is along the way. It's in the doing!

Who will Reform the Clean Air Act?

> —–"The Clean Air Act is complicated, poorly written and rife with contradictions. The only certainty is that if a specific regulation doesn't make sense, then you probably understand it correctly." —
> —-*Robynn Andracsek, Burns & McDonnell*

Who is going to simplify the Clean Air Act? What do we do at our home or job if something needs to be done? Wait for someone else to do it?

It is not our job to modernize the Clean Air Act. We even lack the power, resources, and authority to do this work. The fact though is that it usually is the poor and the weak—and the people whose responsibility it isn't—who we rely upon to get things done in this country. It's just a fact. Always has been.

> —"If you're in trouble, or hurt or need—go to the poor people. They're the only ones that'll help—the only ones."—*John Steinbeck*

And just like the guy that mowed the lawn at the Lincoln Memorial with a push-mower during the government shutdown—doing something that's not

your responsibility and way over your head can have an incredible effect on the people whose responsibility it is.

The world is changing. We must change with it. Time to transform the Clean Air Act. We can make it happen.

What Should We Do?

The ozone standard will be lowered and we will find ourselves repeating history in a procedural morass of administrative exercises and litigation. What should we do? Our choices seem to be to repeat history, wallow in a feeling of helplessness, bury our heads in the sand, criticize the Clean Air Act some more, or try to do something about it. Teddy Roosevelt once wrote the following:

— "It is not the critic who counts, not the man who points out how the strong man stumbled, or where the doer of deeds could have done better. The credit belongs to the man who is actually in the arena, whose face is marred by dust and sweat and blood, who strives valiantly, who errs and comes short again and again, who knows the great enthusiasms, the great devotions, and spends himself in a worthy cause, who at best knows achievement and who at the worst if he fails at least fails while daring greatly so that his place shall never be with those cold and timid souls who know neither victory nor defeat. ---Teddy Roosevelt

We are not cold and timid souls. This is our arena. Let us dare greatly.

Controversy, Conflict, and the Clean Air Act

What a mess huh? The amount of controversy, conflict, and arguing over Clean Air Act matters is deafening . . .almost paralyzing.   Hard not to feel dejected amidst the storm regardless of your perspective.

Just a reminder, as I am also reminding myself, that this too shall pass. All will be well. I was reading the kids "Old Turtle" a while back. In the book the people argue with each other to the point that that which in part they

are arguing over, the earth, begins to die. Eventually though they remember
who they are and their commonality. Here are the last words of the book:

> *"And after a long, lonesome and scary time . . .*
>
> *. . . the people listened, and began to hear . . .*
>
> *And to see God in one another . . .*
>
> *. . . and in the beauty of all the Earth.*
>
> *And Old Turtle smiled.*
>
> *And so did God.*

www.ingramcontent.com/pod-product-compliance
Lightning Source LLC
Chambersburg PA
CBHW060338290526
45793CB00003B/656